MW00905104

LIFELINER

LIFELINER

THE JUDY TAYLOR STORY

SHIREEN JEEJEEBHOY

Ken,
Thank you
for your
help!
Shireen

iUniverse, Inc.
New York Lincoln Shanghai

Lifeliner
The Judy Taylor Story

Copyright © 2007 by Shireen Anne Jeejeebhoy

All rights reserved. No part of this book may be used or reproduced by any means, graphic, electronic, or mechanical, including photocopying, recording, taping or by any information storage retrieval system without the written permission of the publisher except in the case of brief quotations embodied in critical articles and reviews.

iUniverse books may be ordered through booksellers or by contacting:

iUniverse
2021 Pine Lake Road, Suite 100
Lincoln, NE 68512
www.iuniverse.com
1-800-Authors (1-800-288-4677)

Because of the dynamic nature of the Internet, any Web addresses or links contained in this book may have changed since publication and may no longer be valid.

The views expressed in this work are solely those of the author and do not necessarily reflect the views of the publisher, and the publisher hereby disclaims any responsibility for them.

ISBN: 978-0-595-44544-8 (pbk)
ISBN: 978-0-595-68806-7 (cloth)
ISBN: 978-0-595-88872-6 (ebk)

Printed in the United States of America

To
Dreamers broken, who
Remember
Rise
Try again.

Contents

Foreword

by Professor Arvid Wretlind (1919–2002)

Total parenteral nutrition (TPN) has been available for only thirty-odd years. The successful development of this therapy, in a modern sense, was initiated in the late 1930s. However, history in this field goes back more than 350 years.

The first landmark was the description of general blood circulation by William Harvey in 1628. His discovery is the anatomical basis for intravenous infusions. Many investigations were performed during the following centuries showing that solutions containing electrolytes and glucose could be given intravenously in man. The accumulated knowledge of protein metabolism formed the basis for studies on intravenous nutrition with protein hydrolysates, peptides, and amino acids. The observation in the late 1930s by Robert Elman that amino acids in the form of protein hydrolysate could be administered safely in man was the first major step toward TPN. During the following years, major efforts were made to find methods to prepare infusion solutions with a high energy content and low osmotic pressure. The most realistic alternative seemed to be fat in the form of an emulsion. Many studies of a large number of various fat emulsions were made from the 1920s until the end of the 1950s. However, all of these emulsions caused severe adverse reactions in man.

The first safe fat emulsion, Intralipid, was made available in the early 1960s. This was the second major step toward TPN. It was then no problem to include vitamins, electrolytes, and trace elements in the fat emulsions and in the solutions of amino acids and glucose. A few years later, Stanley Dudrick showed that a central venous catheter could be used to administer the infusion fluid intravenously.

Many clinical investigations and reports have shown that the newly developed intravenous nutritional regimens are adequate alternatives to the ordinary diet. In this way, it has been possible to maintain or obtain a good nutritional condition in most situations when oral or tube feeding cannot be used. TPN has been shown to be of very great clinical importance to prevent and treat starvation often related to high morbidity and mortality. The best answers to questions concerning the adequacy of our total intravenous regimen have been given in reports on

patients with the no-bowel syndrome, patients who had been on total intravenous nutrition and had no oral food intake for several years.

The classic case concerns a woman who was treated and investigated by Dr.
Khursheed N. Jeejeebhoy and co-workers. The patient, Mrs. Judy Taylor, was
operated on in September 1970 at the age of thirty-four. A laparotomy disclosed
necrosis of the small and large intestines caused by mesenteric vein thrombosis.
All necrotic intestinal tissue had to be removed, and the patient was left with
merely the stomach and part of the descending colon. Thus, the patient was
unable to resume oral feeding. For this reason, she was given a complete intravenous nutrition, first in the hospital and later in her home. She remained in good
health until March 1991, when she succumbed to an infection unrelated to her
TPN.

There are many patients with similar histories that have been treated with
total intravenous nutrition for several years. This case treated by Dr. Khursheed
Jeejeebhoy was the first showing this therapeutic possibility of complete intravenous nutrition.

I have written many different articles and papers and given a large number of
lectures on parenteral or intravenous nutrition. In all of these, I have mentioned
the names of Dr. Khursheed Jeejeebhoy and Mrs. Judy Taylor several times. Dr.
Khursheed Jeejeebhoy has shown that complete long-term intravenous nutrition
is of great clinical value to maintain a patient in normal condition in a situation
when the patient is unable to use the gastrointestinal tract. Dr. Khursheed Jeejeebhoy must thus be called "the father of complete long-term parenteral nutrition
in man."

I am very glad that this book about Dr. Khursheed Jeejeebhoy and his patient
Mrs. Judy Taylor will be published. In this way, the classic studies will be made
easily available to coming generations.

Acknowledgements

I first met Judy Taylor as a child, when she invited my father—her gastroenterologist—and his family to her home for a barbecue. I will never forget Judy's delicious cookies, an unusual treat for me at the time, or the grin on my father's face as he helped Cliff Taylor, Judy's husband, grill the hamburgers while chatting with his patients. Still, it was not until I was talking to my former boss, Patti Bregman, at Judy's memorial that I became inspired to write Judy's story. I immediately got started on it. However, because of a couple of rather large hiccups, this book took a long time to finish. Each phase of researching and writing brought into my life groups and individuals who helped, encouraged, and supported me. After sixteen years of working on *Lifeliner*, the list of those who assisted me in getting to know Judy and her medical ups and downs is quite extensive, and I am deeply indebted to them all.

But *Lifeliner* would never have gotten off the ground without the help of Judy's family—her husband, Cliff, and her daughters, Cyndy, Julie, and Miriam—my mum and dad, Olive and Khursheed (Jeej) Jeejeebhoy, and my former husband, Normand Landry. Cliff spoke to me for many, many hours about Judy and his life with her; Cyndy was invaluable in helping me to transcribe Judy's huge stacks of medical records at Toronto General Hospital; Dad spent hours telling me about Judy and total parenteral nutrition and explaining all the technical aspects; Julie showed me a different perspective on Judy; and Miriam spent much time and effort not only answering my questions, but also putting me in contact with others who were able to help me.

The now-defunct CPENA (Canadian Parenteral and Enteral Nutrition Association), led by Judy's friend and fellow lifeliner Sandra Lapenny at the time I spoke to Judy's fellow lifeliners about the book, provided the financial support to get me on my way, and its members spent many hours answering my long list of questions. In fact, so many of Judy's friends, fellow patients, and neighbours—and even those who knew her from far-flung places, like her Swedish friends Britt Lindqvist and Ingalill Bergqvist—wanted to tell me about her that I finally had to call a halt, otherwise I might still be interviewing today. To everyone who gave of their time to answer my questions, I thank you so much. (See the back pages for a complete list of people I interviewed and spoke to about Judy.)

The people at the Oley Foundation in New York, in particular Roslyn Dahl, provided me with valuable assistance and leads over the years, and I'm deeply appreciative of all that they did for me.

As I finally saw the end of the research phase, and just before the second hiccup, my former husband and his colleagues held a fundraiser so that I could complete the research, pay for the hundreds of hours of interview transcribing, and begin writing. I was touched and honoured that so many turned out in order to support me financially. To them, I am truly grateful.

The second hiccup, a closed head injury, led me to have to restart the writing of *Lifeliner*. At first, I didn't succeed. After many years of trying and failing, I didn't think it would be possible anymore. But Miriam introduced me to her generous-hearted friend Ian Connerty early in 2006, and he and my structural editor, Greg Ioannou, got me back on track. They made the completion of my manuscript possible. I cannot thank them both enough.

Chapter 1

Back in One Hour

"I'm so lucky to have a family, adopted or not! I'm so lucky to be alive!" Judy Ellis Taylor tells her three school-age girls out of the blue on this chilly September morning. They roll their eyes, having heard this before many a time.

Judy didn't know her biological parents, a twenty-three-year-old nursing-student mother and a twenty-seven-year-old painter father, nor did she care to. To Judy, her real parents were Marjorie and Percy Russell. Shortly after her birth on March 26, 1936, they had scooped up the little round-cheeked, black-haired baby and taken her home. At first, Marjorie hadn't wanted to adopt this baby. Only six months had passed since their second adopted child had died suddenly; but Percy talked to Marjorie gently and persistently until he convinced his devastated wife that she could adopt again, that she could have her dream of children, children who would live. She acquiesced, and they adopted Judy from a Presbyterian home. To help ensure that both their girls, Joyce and Judy, their first and third adopted children, would have the best chance, they moved from Rosedale to a large house in the valley of York Mills, where violets flowed up to the door in springtime. It meant a one-hour drive to his engineering job, but Percy made it sweeter by bringing home chocolate éclairs. Meanwhile, Marjorie anchored their family life with big weekly Sunday lunches after church.

It was a good decision, for Judy thrived on life. She attended the prestigious Bishop Strachan School during her junior-high years and joined the young people's group at St. John's Anglican Church. At thirteen years old, this healthy, mischievous girl pledged herself to Christ at Camp Gay Venture in Haliburton—she didn't explain why to anyone, just did it—and became a camp counsellor at the same time. Like a mother bird, Judy took charge of the little girls at the camp, including Sandra, a small seven-year-old. Judy especially loved teaching the little ones to ride. But being Judy's pupil was not an easy thing: she had a tendency to kick her charges out of the nest if she felt that they could handle it, plus she had a penchant for practical jokes.

One sunny day as the group cantered together, Sandra's black horse (known as Blacky) threw her off. Sandra sniffled on the ground, feeling sorry for herself, while the others milled around. They expected Judy to pick her up, dust her off, and plop her back on her horse. Instead, she steered her horse over and, looking down from her great height, demanded, "Well? What are you going to do about it? I'm going back to the barn. You can either walk or get on your horse and follow me." She gestured to the others to follow her and rode off.

Sandra howled. Some of the kids looked back, but not one slowed down. They disappeared toward the barn. Sandra stopped, mouth open. No point howling anymore. She closed her mouth. She stood up, climbed onto Blacky, and trotted back to camp, where Judy was waiting. "Well, if you hadn't done that, you probably wouldn't ever have ridden again," Judy informed the little girl. "Now take Blacky in and groom her."

That fall, Percy decided that Judy would be better off at his (and my) alma mater, Jarvis Collegiate Institute, near the heart of Toronto, and had her transferred there. She did reasonably well. By age seventeen, she knew what she wanted out of life: to find a husband and have a family.

Judy joined her girlfriends at the church picnic near Fenelon Falls that summer, hoping to find a husband. She did. Her friend introduced her to her boyfriend's buddy. Cliff Taylor was a taciturn, slightly older fellow with a sudden smile and a shock of dark hair. He had to grow up quickly after his mother had tried to kill him along with herself, leaving him alone with his alcoholic father while his younger sister was shipped off to boarding school. By age sixteen, he had dropped out of school to work. He developed a philosophy of paying his own way with cash only. He didn't believe in credit cards or debt, except for a mortgage perhaps. Unlike Judy, he didn't live in the genteel areas of town, but he had become successful in sales and was doing well monetarily. Still, the educated, well-off Judy clicked with this man from the wrong side of the tracks. He loved her with a devotion that drove him to cross the threshold of a church, a feat he vowed never to repeat after their marriage on July 27, 1957, in St. John's Anglican, and she loved him with a strength he could count on.

Cliff bought a new house for his bride, and they settled comfortably into Scarborough life, spending weekends up at the cottage near his father's place in Bobcaygeon, Cliff paying for everything in cash, as usual, and Judy looking after their growing brood: Cyndy, Julie, and Miriam. Judy had grasped her dream. With her family complete, she went on the birth control pill, a fairly new drug back in late 1966. She was wildly happy and having fun.

But God wasn't impressed with Judy's life plan. He gave her the gifts of toughness, generosity, kindness, healing, advocacy, and teaching. Her dream was too mundane for those gifts, and He would call her to travel to unfamiliar places, places so dark, frightening, and unexpected that she would have no choice but to trust in His faithfulness to her.

Stomach pain was the first intimation of the change to come. The stomach pain was so bad that, after three months, it forced her to see her general practitioner (GP) in February 1967. Despite X-rays, blood tests, and referrals to specialists, nothing revealed the source of her pain, although by 1970 her insatiable appetite and loss of weight clued one of her specialists, a gastroenterologist, into the fact that she might have hyperthyroidism. She joked to her girls that she could run up and down the road at ninety miles an hour, making them laugh while she hid from them the wrenching pain deep inside her. By the summer of 1970, her endocrinologist irradiated her thyroid. Perhaps things would settle down now, Judy and Cliff hoped.

But the pain squeezed harder. Her doctor prescribed morphine; Cliff and Judy hid that, too, from their girls, or so they thought. Family conversations took a strange turn. The talkative, joking Judy suddenly would stop mid-sentence; they would all pretend she hadn't and would gamely continue on the conversation without her. Suddenly, she'd pop back up and finish her sentence. Unfortunately, she would soon space out again, and cries of "Mom? Mom!" from her girls would go unheeded. Frightened, the three dared not ask about this phenomenon when she resurfaced from wherever she'd been, and they pretended that everything was normal. Judy had deceived herself into thinking they hadn't noticed, clenching her teeth against the truth, fighting both the pain and the effects of the morphine.

Wednesday, September 23, 1970, dawns cold. The pain had increased during the past weekend. She had spent the time at the cottage, lying balled up on her bed while the children played with their dog, Goldie, under the sunny fall skies. Back at home, she had pushed herself to get through Monday and Tuesday, but today, Wednesday, she calls her GP. With Cliff by her side, she dials his number. He's on vacation. His partner takes her early morning call. He instructs her to call her endocrinologist, the one who irradiated her thyroid. She calls him, but her symptoms are outside his field of specialty, he informs her. She hangs up frustrated and decides to soldier on. "I'll be fine," she assures Cliff so that he will leave for work and not worry about her. She has toughed it out for over three years; one more day will not be so hard.

But Cliff feels unconvinced. He writes down his work number and commands her to call him.

Later that morning, after her family has left, Judy's neighbour Frances comes over for their usual cup of tea and chat. After one look at Judy, Frances runs to fetch her next-door neighbour Fran. They return to find Judy lying on the chesterfield, wearing shorts and shivering. Fran dashes into the bedroom and grabs a pair of slacks and a blanket. Judy—the one who always does things for herself, who never discusses her health, who never talks of her ailment—now lets her two neighbours bundle her up.

Fran asks her, "Where's the pain?"

Judy points to, but dares not touch, her sore stomach and confesses her whole story.

Fran thinks that maybe it's appendicitis and is livid at the doctor's inane advice. They should call Cliff, she asserts, and she takes the slip of paper with his work number on it and calls while Frances offers Judy some tea.

Judy cannot abide the thought and turns her head away. Fran suggests that she make lunch for Judy's girls at her place. Judy nods.

Frances has to go back home, but Fran stays. Judy feels maybe a visit to the bathroom will help. She rises carefully from the chesterfield and leans gratefully on her neighbour's arm for the short walk down the hallway. But the bathroom visit doesn't help. The pain hangs on, her nerves screech at her every movement. She lies back down on the chesterfield with relief.

It's eleven o'clock. The phone rings. Fran picks it up. It's Cliff, calling her back. "I may be wrong, but that wouldn't cause what she had, right?" she asks him, referring to Judy's hyperthyroidism.

Cliff doesn't know; he says it's all incomprehensible to him, this illness stuff.

Fran gets off the phone as lunch is fast approaching. She has to get it ready and bake cookies for her son and for Judy's three girls. "I'll ask Frances to keep an eye on you till after lunch," she tells Judy. She runs out the door under the scudding clouds and light rain to Frances's place. Although Frances has her own four kids to make lunch for, she pops over several times and takes messages from a worried Cliff. He's coming home early, and she lets Fran know this when she returns after lunch.

At 5:30 PM, Cliff barrels in from work. He watches Fran leave with a worried backward glance at Judy. He unwraps the fish 'n chips he'd picked up on his way home and coaxes his wife to eat at least a little bit. Fish 'n chips. The last meal of her life. If only they had known, he would've gotten something nicer.

Fed and off the couch, Judy takes a deep breath and throws her affliction out of her mind. Life cannot stop just because my innards are screaming, she thinks. Her girls need new running shoes, groceries need to be bought, for it's Wednesday night, grocery night. She tells Cliff to get the car ready, and she steels herself for the drive to Parkway Plaza. There in the middle of the grocery store, she sways.

Cliff grabs her and half carries half walks her to the car with the girls running along beside them. Cliff rushes them home and settles his wife on the chesterfield. He whips across the street to ask Frances if she can look after the children while he takes Judy to the doctor's office.

Frances doesn't hesitate to say yes, and the two race back to his house. They wrap Judy up in blankets.

As Cliff carries her out the door to the car, Judy—ever protective and still trying to hide her illness—calls back to her girls: "We're just going to the doctor's. We'll be back in an hour."

Chapter 2

Shunts!

Saliva and blood spew out as the man coughs, startling his father, doctor, and nurses.

"I can't breathe!"

Dr. Khursheed N. Jeejeebhoy picks up the man's wrist, feels his rapid pulse, sees the sweat bead out on his forehead, and knows. Damn. His patient is throwing clots, probably from his ulnar veins where the shunt is implanted, and forming pulmonary emboli. They are killing him. Quickly, he directs the residents and nurses to action to try to dissolve these clots, but it's 1970, and treatment options are limited. Fury fills him at this unnecessary complication. The shunt is supposed to save his patient's life, not kill him. This kind of medicine is not what he has been raised to do.

Jeejeebhoy started his journey to practising medicine in Toronto as a junior gastroenterologist at Toronto General Hospital (TGH) on August 26, 1935, in Rangoon, Burma. The first living child born to a prosperous lawyer and a musically talented mother and the grandson of lawyers and doctors, he spent his first seven years learning from his devoted maternal grandparents and being cosseted by the servants. His only sister died at eighteen months of a fit. After more miscarriages, his mother once again became successfully pregnant with his only brother. At the same time, the Japanese invaded Burma, causing the entire family to flee to India in 1942—his father with the army overland and him, his pregnant mother, and maternal grandmother, along with a motley group of refugees, in a Dakota airplane flown by Chinese pilots. As they approached the Burma-India border, the Indian Air Force flew out to fight off the Japanese attackers. He went from a cushy life to an uncertain, nomadic one in India; he determined to become self-sufficient. He also decided to follow in his grandmother's footsteps. He had the innate talent, and she had instilled in him good work habits and taught him that his Zoroastrian faith required him to always look for the divine in his decisions, to think good thoughts so that his words would be good, and to speak good words so that his words would lead to good actions, actions that would help and heal his fellow human beings.

He shot through school quickly, passed the equivalent of grade-thirteen final exams at thirteen years old, and was admitted to Christian Medical College in Vellore, India, at such a young age that he had to study economics and political science for two years in university before being old enough to commence his medical studies. He briefly flirted with surgery—but surgeons have to start too early in the day for his taste—before settling on gastroenterology. He earned his PhD at London University in England and met my mother, his future wife, at West Middlesex Hospital, where he was a house officer. They met because she got salmonella poisoning (not for the last time), and he was the one tasked to tend her. I was born a week before their first anniversary; three months later, we were sailing for Bombay, India, where he intended to set up his practice. But life in India was not as he had envisioned it. The political atmosphere and restrictions chafed on him; a doctor from Canada, on sabbatical in Bombay, noticed and recommended him to Dr. Keith J. R. Wightman, Chair of the Department of Medicine at the University of Toronto and Physician-in-Chief at TGH, as a man well suited for Wightman's burgeoning gastroenterology department. All of a sudden, we—Jeejeebhoy (my father), my mother, my four-month-old brother, and I—were moving to Toronto, Canada. My father struggled from 1968 to 1970 to build up a practice at TGH as only the second non–Anglo Saxon staff member, after his surgical colleague Dr. Bernard (Bernie) Langer. As the newbie, he got the tough cases, the ones no one else wanted, like this man dying before him now.

This man had been shuffled over to him because of his difficult condition: pseudo-obstruction. This ailment of the gut looks like a physically obstructed bowel but is not; still, it prevents the patient from digesting his food. Far from being daunted, Jeejeebhoy relished the challenge this man brought, and he desired to send his patient home healthy.

When reviewing the case, he had realized that his new patient needed to be nourished for a long time through some method other than eating. The problem was that the current short-term artificial feeding he was using on Langer's post-operative patients would be insufficient. Looking for better methods of treating him, he talked to colleagues and then thumbed through the literature until he found a research paper in the prestigious *Journal of the American Medical Association* by Dr. Belding Scribner. Scribner described a new way to artificially feed people beyond the current standard of just a few days. He wrote that he had adapted his shunt—a silicone rubber and Teflon, U-shaped device that allowed

for continuing arteriovenous access for kidney dialysis and that had revolutionized the field of home hemodialysis—to feed people a nutritional solution. He
called it an artificial gut. Gastroenterologists around the world had been racing
after the holy grail of artificial feeding, trying to overcome many problems,
including the very big one of how to infuse a solution permanently through a
vein, and here Scribner seemed to have found it. Jeejeebhoy wasn't completely
convinced about its efficacy, but in consulting with senior colleagues, he was
advised to try it on this patient dying of pseudo-obstruction.

And now, his patient is dying from the shunt. The man moans and grabs his
chest. He loses consciousness. He dies. A cry rises from the corner where his
father has been standing out of the way of those struggling to save his son's life.
He turns on Jeejeebhoy, demanding to know why the gastroenterologist has just
let his son die.

Why did he have to use this technology, this shunt? Why did he have to die? Jeejeebhoy wants to know that, too. He tries to comfort the father, but the man has
already turned his back, collapsing at the side of his dead son's bed. Jeejeebhoy
watches for a moment, compresses his lips, turns on his heels, and strides out of
the room to the nurses' station where he meets up with Pat Walker, the head
nurse who is thrilled to be working with and learning from such a talented physician, and with Langer. He tells them what has just happened. He cannot believe
it. He had followed a leading researcher's findings to the letter, and it has killed
his patient. His patient!

Jeejeebhoy fumes silently for a moment and then declares, "We cannot use
this shunt again. I won't have my patients dying on me. We have to go back to
the central line. We'll just have to start from scratch and do our own thing." He
stalks back to his office.

Chapter 3

Surgeries and Starvation

The black night envelops the car as it hisses along the road toward Judy and Cliff's family doctor. But he's away. Instead, his partner examines Judy, quickly covers her back up, and tells them that she needs to go to Scarborough General Hospital now. She has to see the gynecologist on call. Luckily, the hospital is just across the road.

Within minutes, Cliff has helped Judy into an examining room and up onto the bed, and the gynecologist is examining her. After the gynecologist straightens up, he says that in his considered opinion, Judy has a torsion of an ovarian cyst, which needs to be operated upon directly. "Go home," he tells Cliff. "I'll call you when we're done." As Cliff drives home, the specialist admits Judy for a laparotomy.

In the operating room, with the GP assisting him, he cuts Judy open, but to his surprise, finds nothing wrong in the pelvis. It's late, and the organs above the pelvis are outside his area of expertise. He could close up and leave it for the general surgeon to explore in a day or two, but this young mother needs help now, plus he doesn't want to put her through the stress of an incomplete operation followed by another operation in a day or two. He's also puzzled by what is causing her excruciating pain and is concerned that she might not survive it for another day. He explores upward.

He removes her healthy appendix, which is standard operating procedure in 1970, and then examines her ileum, a lower part of the bowel, and finds the problem. Ten centimetres from the cecum, about a half-inch of the bowel has died due to a lack of blood supply. He excises the pale tissue and inspects the rest of the bowel to ensure that there is adequate blood supply. It's pink. He's relieved. He stitches the two ends of the bowel back together, closes the incision, sends her to recovery, and calls Cliff with the good news at one o'clock in the morning.

Cliff is elated. Someone has finally rid Judy of her terrible pain. She will return to him. Things will go back to normal. His broad smile beams his relief to Fran, who had taken over from Frances and is keeping him company. He and Fran chatter about what has happened and reassure themselves that Judy won't miss such a small piece of bowel; after all, the bowel is extremely long. The only thing that now worries Cliff is what to tell the children in the morning before they leave for school. Fran suggests saying that the surgeon removed her appendix. That should be light enough not to frighten them. He agrees. And he knows Judy would agree, too.

The days slip by as Judy seems to heal. A Penrose drain attached to a noisy pump speeds up the process by suctioning fluid and infection from her abdomen. But she starts to feel the old pain again, on top of the post-surgical pain. Worse, large amounts of cells and pus start flowing out of her drain. The surgeons discuss this worrying turn. Perhaps the sutures tying the two ends of her bowel together have come apart, causing the bowel contents to leak out into her abdominal cavity and on out through the drain.

A new surgeon examines Judy on September 28, one who knows more about operating on the intestines than the first guy. She is moaning and semi-conscious from the pain. Dr. Michael O'Dwyer decides to X-ray her the next day and operate again. He has the staff inform Cliff.

The X-ray reveals a scary story: her intestines are paralysed and are not working. Judy is wheeled back into the operating room on September 30. O'Dwyer slices her skin, revealing a nice pink peritoneum. So far, things look normal. He slices through the covering over the intestines, and shock halts his hand. Fecal-stained and bloody fluid has flooded her insides from her diaphragm to her pelvis. He gingerly touches the small bowel, now grey-white in colour instead of its usual red. It falls apart. Frowning, he looks at the gall bladder. Its wall is necrotic, and bile has stained it and has spilled onto the stomach, the duodenum, and the liver. He notices a number of yellow-grey patches on the liver surface; later, as the surgery continues, he notices that they are increasing. Wondering how and where the blood flow has stopped, he first feels the pulse of the superior mesenteric artery, the main source of blood supply for the bowels. Nothing. Then he feels the celiac artery. Nothing. The hepatic artery. Nothing. The splenic artery. Again, no pulse. Hesitantly, he checks the aorta. It is pulsing away. Relief. Next, he examines the colon, the large part of the bowel, and tries to mobilize it. But here, too, gangrene has set in. He absorbs this information. From the fourth portion of her duodenum all the way down to the cecum, her bowels are dead, and her omentum, the fat that sits underneath the stomach, is greyish green and lifeless. The contents spilling out of her bowels and the dead tissue have created a rampant infection inside her abdomen. She's finished.

Still, something moves him to believe that life is possible and not to sew her back up with autopsy stitches and send her back to her room to die.

With his scalpel, he swiftly excises thirty-two feet of dead bowel from the third portion of the duodenum to just above the rectum, as well as the gall bladder. He ties off the cystic artery just in case blood flow returns and it starts to bleed. He hunts for the clot that has created this mess and finds it in the superior mesenteric vein—with blood unable to flow out of the digestive system through this vein, it had backed up into the arteries. Eventually, circulation had stopped altogether. That's how the gangrene had set in. He puts in a one-inch Penrose drain, attempts to stitch the two far-apart stumps of bowel together, stitches her wound up, and sends her to recovery. Now, for the hard part.

"We found a previously healthy bowel grey and friable," he explains to Cliff later in Judy's room so that both can hear the news in person instead of over the impersonal phone. Judy seems comatose. "We had to excise her intestines from the duodenum down to her descending colon. Unfortunately, Mr. Taylor, your wife cannot live without bowels. We will, of course, keep her comfortable."

Cliff reels. Judy cannot die. This crisis is all supposed to be over.

She moans. The pain is flowing over her stomach, and she's thirsty. She begs the surgeon not to let her die. "I can't die! I can't leave yet. You have to do something, anything, to save me."

The surgeon shakes his head sorrowfully and leaves. All they can do is infuse her with IV glucose and morphine to keep her comfortable until she dies of starvation.

He goes to the coffee room, hoping for some solace, and relates this sad story to his colleagues. One volunteers that he's heard of a young gastroenterologist downtown doing some sort of work on new feeding technology. Maybe he can help. Anything is worth a try, he thinks. His patient badly wants to live, and her husband already looks lost. He calls the gastroenterologist. Well, the young man asserts, they are not quite ready to try long-term alimentation in the hospital again, never mind in a way that will allow the patient to go home, but he's willing to try since she wants to live. "Sure, send her over."

With guarded hope, O'Dwyer tells the Taylors of this possible lifeline. "She might have a chance with this doctor," he tells Cliff. Judy hears and decides. She has to go.

Chapter 4

Dr. Cowboy

"I have no problem going in the ambulance. You turn that light on, you turn that siren on, you're to stop, pull over, and let me out!" Judy is not too happy about all this dramatic fuss over her. The ambulance attendants ignore Judy's outraged wails, expertly push her stretcher into the vehicle, and slam the doors shut. Inside the artificially lit, cramped space, the frosted, white-lined windows shut out the night, but the doors at Judy's feet menace her with the possibility of flying open, of sucking her and her stretcher out onto the road as they race down the Don Valley Parkway, known colloquially as the Parkway, to TGH. She passes out and comes to in her new room.

Putrid green walls stare back at her as she looks around wondering where she is. She's off the stretcher and in a new, proper hospital bed, but the same wad of stained bandages cover up her wound. The same sickly sweet smell perfumes the air. The same warm ooze is slipping over her stomach. Shoes squeak toward her, and she turns her head to see a stocky man with skin the colour of milk chocolate and straight, thick, black hair cut short on the back and sides. He's dressed in a blue shirt, blue pants, and a striped tie, but no white coat. Standing at her bedside, he pronounces his name. "I'm Dr. Jeejeebhoy."

A cowboy? A cowboy is her new doctor? "Jeejee," she guffaws.

Suddenly, she fears that the hospital is going to kick her out. A horse is looking after her, so they are going to kick her out. She screams for Cliff, who hears her as he is racing down the hallway looking for her. Jeejeebhoy leaves to search for her husband.

Cliff rushes in and grabs her hand. "They're kicking me out. You have to stop them!" she screams. She can't leave! This is the place they'd sent her to save her life!

"*Shhh*," he comforts her. "They won't. I've bought the place. It's yours, and you can stay as long as you want."

Relieved, she stops. Of course, Cliff will take care of her. She tells him about Dr. Cowboy.

Cliff is puzzled. "Who's Dr. Cowboy?" he asks.

"Jee, jee, jee, jee … a horse." She sees the cowboy doctor pop back in, followed by a bunch of young men and a nice-looking woman. She points him out to Cliff. "Jeejee!"

He introduces himself. "I'm Dr. Jeejeebhoy. Is she always like this?" he asks Cliff. "Is she ever sensible?"

"It's the morphine."

He nods and then turns to Judy. In an uncompromising tone, he tells her that he has to examine her to see what they are dealing with. She acquiesces. He undresses her stomach, and the smell of rotting meat grows. His face turns grave. A yellowish liquid is eating her skin. Brown muck and blood ooze between the open stitches that had been laced up the middle of her stomach; only her pleura forms a protective barrier between her innards and the air outside. Tubes emerge from around the hole. The resident beside him can hear faint bowel sounds even though the bowels supposedly have been removed. Her skin is puckered, dried up, and pale. No wonder it cannot hold the stitches. In the quiet, as the gastroenterologist and his residents contemplate what they see, Judy turns to Cliff and begs him not to let her die.

Then she turns to Jeejee, her new cowboy doctor, and begs him not to let her die.

"I have three girls," she tells him. "Who will look after Cliff and my girls if I die? I have to live. I want to live." She turns to her husband. "He has to understand that," she says. "I can't stay in the hospital. I can't die," she pleads again with this specialist. He looks right at her with his intense, cocoa-coloured eyes and nods. She falls back onto her pillows and closes her own hazel eyes. He carefully redresses her and then turns to his residents, while Pat, standing nearby, listens as well. He orders cultures of her wound and urine as well as blood tests. He wants her put on ampicillin until they get the cultures back and know precisely what bacteria they are dealing with, and he wants her on 50 mg Demerol every six hours to curb her agony while reducing the hallucinations from the morphine. He instructs Pat to put her on IV fluids to rehydrate her and give her ice chips for her dry mouth. Water is too dangerous for her to drink; in her semi-comatose state, she might choke on it. He tells Cliff that he doesn't know if he can keep her alive, but he'll try. Then he leaves.

His staff scurries around, carrying out his orders, while he spends the rest of the night reading up on nutritional research. Judy has arrived rather too suddenly for him to know what and how to feed her: short-term patients in the hospital hadn't necessarily needed complete nutrition, but this lady will, as she cannot take anything by mouth; the temporary catheters they currently use will be no good in the long term; and that shunt was a complete failure. He needs to decide what and how to nourish her before talking it over with the pharmacist in the morning.

Meanwhile, the first order of business for the residents is to drain her stomach acid to stop it from leaking onto her skin and burning her. A young man in a white coat with a large snake in his hand approaches Judy's bed. He explains, in case she comprehends, "We're going to put in an NG tube. You'll hardly feel it." While the nurse stands next to him, he sticks the snake up one of her nostrils.

The pain of it snaps her eyes open, and she becomes frantic. He tells her to calm down and again explains this is to help her.

When she seems calmer, he continues pushing it up her nose until it hits the top with a painful lurch, and then he snakes it down toward the back of her throat, at which point he orders her to swallow. Judy seems perplexed. "You won't choke. Swallow." She swallows. The nasogastric tube slides down her esophagus and into her stomach. He tapes it to the side of her nose and her face so that she won't pull it out.

He leaves, and Pat catheterizes her urinary tract. She hooks the catheter up to a bag attached to the side of the bed. And when Judy calls out for water, she gives her ice chips to suck on and keeps an eye on her. The cool wetness soothes Judy's mouth. Once she's finished them, Pat fetches an IV kit, punctures her arm, and hooks her up to an IV bottle on a pole next to the bed. Glucose and ampicillin flow into her vein. Finally, she injects her with Demerol. Judy falls asleep. Cliff walks out of her room to head for home, his head down, his feet dragging. He is afraid.

Chapter 5

Garbage-Bag Dressings

It's been thirteen days since Judy's last meal. Her body has cannibalized her fat and muscle for nourishment, but it's not enough to feed her brain. She speaks slowly with effort. Her liver is sluggish. Her skin is inelastic. It and the whites of her eyes are yellow; her urine is tea coloured. She is starving to death.

At home, Jeejee considers the problem. What food do people require? How best can I help her? She needs something for life, something to mimic real food, not something that will make do for a couple of weeks. A normal diet comprises protein, carbohydrates, fat, vitamins, trace elements, and electrolytes. That's the combination she needs, yet he wonders how he'll give her fat. American and Swedish researchers have been warring over which fat is best for IV infusion and whether one needs fat at all. The Americans shun fat, for the product that they had devised had proven toxic, and they believe it makes the liver fatty. But the latter doesn't make sense to him. Fat is in our diet for a reason—and Judy cannot go a lifetime without it. He rereads the papers published by Prof. Arvid Wretlind of the Karolinska Institute in Sweden. Wretlind has developed soybean-oil-based IV fat emulsion, which has been used in Europe for several years. He decides that he will use this fat emulsion. Still, he wonders, will it lead to fatty liver? He has a theory about that.

Now for the next decision: which trace elements shall he give Judy? He pulls out animal studies from his stack of literature. Because veterinary science is often ahead of human science, these studies are often more informative. He peruses his stack of journals late into the night until he's satisfied that he has a viable plan. He retires to bed.

Early the next morning of Wednesday, October 7, Jeejee visits Dieter Baun, the hospital pharmacist, in the basement of TGH. They discuss what to feed Judy. Baun had turned the hospital pharmacy into a sterile production centre for sterile solutions when Jeejee and Langer had first started working with hyperalimentation (or nutritional IV solution) for their post-operative, short-term patients. Thus, he is already set up to create Judy's alimentation that day. They decide to customize commercial solutions by injecting the nutrients they specifically want into the ready-made bags. This method will speed up the process of manufacturing Judy's alimentation. Satisfied that Baun has things under control, Jeejee leaves for G South, the ward Judy is on, to arrange for a way to get the alimentation into Judy's veins.

Since the fiasco with the Scribner shunt, Jeejee has reverted to using temporary catheters because they're the fastest and most proven way to infuse alimentation. But these catheters are problematic. Because they're made of plastic, they not only fall out easily, but they also stimulate tissue reaction, allowing clots to form on the inside of the tubing, clogging it up. The catheters become unusable after only a few days and need to be replaced. If this feeding succeeds, they will have to look for a better type of line. But that's in the future. For now, Jeejee calls in a respirologist to insert the plastic catheter.

The respirologist swabs Judy's chest and punctures it as she lies semi-conscious in her hospital bed. He feeds the thin, clear tubing into her vein until its tip reaches her heart. Suddenly, Judy cannot breathe; she sucks air in and out, in and out, in and out. Swiftly, he stabs her chest, slips a tube through the hole and down between her ribs to the area around her lungs, and attaches it to a machine to suck out the air that's squeezing her lung and pushing her trachea to the right. He leaves the tube in until the hole heals shut. Her trachea takes until seven o'clock in the evening to shift back into place. Still, her temporary catheter is in, and he tells the resident that they can start running the alimentation, which has already arrived on the floor from the pharmacy.

Pat knows the routine from their experiments on post-operative patients. She hangs the alimentation bags on Judy's IV pole. She enrobes them in big, black blood-pressure cuffs. She connects the bags one to the other with tubing, leaving the last tube hanging down, its end capped. She pressurizes the cuffs, lets the alimentation flow down to the end cap, pulls the pole closer to Judy, uncaps the end piece of tubing, and connects it to the catheter sticking out of Judy's chest after first ensuring it is clear of debris. She watches the alimentation flow down the tubing and into Judy for several minutes. Satisfied that there are no clots, she leaves. Later, she comes in to find Judy smiling. She has a nice buzz going.

Pat smiles back at Judy's questioning face. "It's the alcohol," Pat explains. Then she tells Judy a story. Jeejee's lab partner at the University of Toronto, ABR (as everyone calls Alan Bruce-Robertson), was looking for subjects to test how alcohol in IV form affects humans. Pat had volunteered. She wanted to be a part of Jeejee's fascinating research. ABR asked her about her drinking habits to determine her suitability as a test subject before he signed her up. Unfortunately, she'd made the mistake of thinking her definition of being a drinker was the same as his, and if she'd also known that ABR starts his mornings boiling his coffee on the stove and drinking it straightaway in one gulp and prescribes the most wickedly effective cough syrups, she might've had second thoughts. As it was, he hooked her up, and she was soon giggling and lolling about. There was no way she could get home on her own, and so he loaded her up into the back of his station wagon and drove her home. She was sick for a week.

Between the story, the buzz, and the Demerol, Judy laughs helplessly. But a few hours later, she has a hangover. She and Pat agree that she cannot go through life drunk. But for now, the alcohol acts as a little calorie packer, and Jeejee will find a better solution down the road.

After she finishes her story, Pat gets up and rubs Judy's legs. She moves them up and down, bending and straightening first her left leg and then her right, in order to get the blood circulating. It soothes Judy, and she falls asleep.

Pat contemplates that horrid wound. How are they going to dress that big hole so that it stops leaking? She talks it over with some of the other nurses, and they come up with a novel idea: they'll dress her in garbage bags. Since it's time to change Judy's soaked and stained dressing, they'll do it now.

Pat carefully peels off the old dressings. She cleans the wound and packs in some gauze. One of the nurses has found some green garbage bags. Pat lays these over her stomach and over her dressings. They slide off. She asks another nurse to get some special tape, and while she holds the garbage bags in place, the nurse straps them on with three or four adhesive straps, which the nurses then lace up.

Judy wakes up, looks down at what they've done, and giggles. She's wearing a green garbage-bag corset! The nurses laugh with her and tell her that, since she no longer leaks, they can move her to a chair. This will keep her muscles and blood moving.

They sit Judy up, swing her legs over the side of the bed, pause to let her catch her breath, and then help her stand up. With Pat on one side and a nurse on the other, they coax her to head toward the chair. She's so tired and in pain that she doesn't want to move. They encourage her and gently, step by step, walk her to the chair and lower her down. Pat sits beside her and talks to her while holding her hand. It comforts Judy.

Judy looks out the window and sees a tree, the tree that Cliff will come to park under when he visits her every night. Its vibrant leaves against the deep blue autumn sky connect her back to life. She breathes it in. Her body slowly sinks in on itself.

Pat pats her hand to tell her it's time to return to bed and undergo her hourly dressing change. Once Judy is back in bed, the nurses put on a new garbage-bag dressing, prop a sheet tent over her torso to give her some dignity, check her alimentation, and then leave her to sleep for a bit. She sleeps fitfully.

Cliff walks in, the first visit of many, afraid of what he will find. He's not yet used to this new reality. He sits next to her and takes her hand in his. He broods. Jeejee had told him that if Judy can survive all the surgeries to come, then he can probably keep her alive on his feeding system. But Cliff wonders what the future will bring. The evening drags until it's time for him to return home.

Judy wakes up to see Cyndy, Julie, and Miriam climbing up and down the tree outside her window, grabbing the branches to pull themselves up or swing down. Every so often, they stop, point at Judy, and laugh. Horror and shame fill her, and she starts to cry. Suddenly, they rise up at the end of her bed, peeping at her. Then just as suddenly, they disappear. She looks around fearfully, but she's free of the hallucination. She falls asleep.

Chapter 6

Let Judy Die

Judy's mother sits beside her, as she has every day, watching the daughter who was not supposed to die dying. She sees her daughter lying semi-conscious in the stark hospital bed under a sheet tent, smelling like rot, looking emaciated. Tubes are coming out of her from everywhere, and pumps are all around. She cannot see how her daughter will live. She misses her lively daily telephone calls.

Only a month ago, she and Judy spoke every morning on the telephone, talking about her grandchildren, talking about Cliff, talking about things a mother and daughter are supposed to talk about. With Percy having died in 1963 from a heart attack, the phone calls had become even more important to her. But now, she sits in silence beside her silent, still daughter in the midst of the noisy machines keeping Judy alive. This is their new morning ritual.

Every morning, Marjorie eats breakfast, gets dressed, and goes down to TGH to sit in this green room with her dying daughter. Meanwhile, her daughter, who speaks little and hardly knows that her mother is there, doesn't eat breakfast and doesn't need to get dressed. Marjorie hates this new morning ritual.

Suddenly, she has had enough. She stands up, picks up her purse, and walks out of the room and down the hallway to the gastroenterologist's office. Sun streams in through the window behind the cheerful young secretary. The blue-walled waiting room is empty. She asks to see Dr. Jeejeebhoy and is told he will be coming out of his office soon. She sits down. A strange-looking calendar with odd caricatures all over it leers down at her from the wall. She stares into space, seeing the image of her dying daughter, steeling herself against tears. Men don't like weepy women.

He comes out with a patient, sees her, and comes over.

"Hello, Mrs. Russell. What can I do for you?"

"I need to talk to you."

"Certainly," he says and leads her into his office.

He gestures toward a chair, but she cannot sit. She's too pent up to sit and blurts out her thoughts. "Dr. Jeejeebhoy, my daughter is dying. It is not possible to live without eating. And with no bowels, she cannot eat! I don't understand what it is that you're doing, but my daughter isn't getting any better. Let her die. For pity's sake, let her die in peace."

"Mrs. Russell, I am trying to save her life. I agree, we're trying new technology, and I don't know if it will work, but she wants to live, and as long as she wants to live, I have to give her that chance."

"I watched one daughter die already. I cannot watch another."

"This must be very difficult for you. But I will do everything I can to make sure she doesn't die. We're giving her the best of care here."

She doesn't speak for a moment. Then she nods and walks out. He follows her, reaching round to open the outside door for her as she exits to the hallway, where she pauses and turns back to face him. "Please let her die," she says, but her plea is a token effort. She knows she cannot change his mind, or Judy's.

He watches her walk back to G South and to her vigil.

"Khush, I want to talk to you about this patient I hear you've taken on."

Hearing his name, he looks around to see one of his senior colleagues descending upon him.

"What you're doing to this poor woman is barbaric, sticking her with needles, putting tubes down her throat. You don't really think this is going to work. It's all very well for you and Bernie to feed post-operative patients this way, you can't do much harm in the short term, but for heaven's sake, man, this is insanity."

He bristles. "I've worked with Dieter in mixing solutions that will properly nourish her. I can feed her. I've proven that already. The only problem is how to infuse it long term, to find a catheter that will stay in, and Bernie is working on that."

"You have to stop this nonsense Khush. You're being presumptuous, playing God like this. She's going to die, and nothing you can do will save her. You're merely prolonging the inevitable."

He tightens his lips. "I have patients to see on the ward."

"I'll walk with you." The two men walk the short distance to the G South nurses' station, which faces Judy's room. They stop at the counter. The senior colleague continues, "Look, you're still new here, so I give you that you may be able to feed her, maybe, but that infection I hear she has, that will surely kill her. And you'll have wasted money and valuable hospital resources on her. But even if you can save her, what kind of life will she have? You can't expect a once-healthy, vital woman to put up with the life of an invalid. She will be subnormal. That's no way to live. Be realistic man."

"All right. I'll see if she can fight off the infection on her own. I won't do any heroic measures. But we'll continue to feed her."

His colleague smiles, slaps him on the shoulder, and says, "That's my man." He hasn't looked once into Judy's room from their vantage point across the hall. The colleague retraces his steps back out of the ward while the young gastroenterologist looks across the hall into Judy's room, where he sees her holding onto Cliff's hand tightly.

Her voice rises above the sound of the pumps. "Cliff, please don't let me die!"

Chapter 7

"I Could Be Pushing Up Daisies"

"Oh, God! Not again!" Judy protests to Pat as she comes in with a tray. "You took some this morning."

"Now, you know he needs these blood tests to tweak your food."

"I'm just a pincushion to Jeej," Judy groans, using her new, shortened nickname for Jeejeebhoy.

"Well, if your veins would stay open for us, we wouldn't have to prick you three times a day!"

"I dare you to find a vein," Judy taunts back as she sticks out her arm with its papery yellow skin and lines of needle tracks. Pat takes it and taps till she finds a vein. She loops the tourniquet around Judy's upper arm and ties it tight. Judy winces. They both watch her blue vein swell until Pat slowly, slowly punctures her skin, trying not to hurt her. With agonizing slowness, blood flows, maroon and thick, into the clear glass. Once all the samples are taken, she snaps off the tourniquet, tapes cotton wool over the puncture mark, sweeps up the needle and vials onto the tray, and hurries out. Judy calls hoarsely after her for ice. Getting blood taken is thirsty work.

Judy runs her tongue over her cracked lips. She worries her loose, gummy teeth and gingerly pokes at her sore gums. Her breath parches her tongue. "Ice," she croaks again. Suddenly, the cup is in her hand. She sucks and sucks; the ice chips melt in the hot confines of her mouth and are gone. Pat takes the cup from her and places a tray of Q-Tips and bottles on the nightstand. She pours hydrogen peroxide on a Q-Tip and sticks it in Judy's mouth, running it over her gums and teeth. Judy grimaces at the solution's bite. Still, it cleanses the stale thickness. Pat soaks another Q-Tip with glycerine. She sticks the Q-Tip in Judy's mouth, rubbing the inside cheeks, gums, teeth, and tongue with moisture. Judy sighs in relief and falls asleep.

Pat lets her rest for a while, but it's soon time to inject vitamins into her buttocks. These vitamins, suspended in oil, cannot go in her alimentation. Pat lifts the sheet, checks the spray from the needle, and jabs it into one of Judy's hips. Judy yelps. The oily emulsion pools for a while inside her muscle before ever so slowly being absorbed. That's painful. Very painful. But she smiles, just as she does through dressing changes, endless blood tests, alimentation changes, catheter cleanings, catheter replacements, drainage tubes, injections. Pain means life. And if she can endure all this, then Jeej will save her.

Meanwhile, Jeej has kept his word. He administered no antibiotics for four days, and far from keeling over, Judy's powerful immune system battled the bacteria eating away at her innards, cooling her fever and rehydrating her body. Judy wants to live, unquestionably. He has her permission—the only one that counts—to do everything possible to save her life. There is nothing dignified about dying without putting up a fight for life.

Jeej consults with an infectious diseases (ID) specialist, and they decide to try a course of massive antibiotic therapy. But the therapy has no effect on the aggressive bugs. He and the ID specialist stop the therapy. They'll have to rely on the drains to siphon the bacteria out of her. She is reaching the critical point: either the bacteria will kill her, or she will kill them.

To see what's going on inside her, Jeej orders a gastrographic X-ray. Judy tolerates the contrast she must swallow, and the X-ray goes well. He and Langer study the film and do not like what they see. Duodenal and descending colon fistulae—holes from the bowel stumps to the skin—riddle her abdomen.

Jeej goes to speak to Judy. "We have the results back. You have a free and wide opening from your duodenum into your peritoneum. The anastomosis has broken down." Judy blinks. "What this means is that the two free ends of your bowels are emptying their contents into your body." She stares at him. "You understand?" She nods. "This is why you have a massive infection. The massive therapy isn't working, so we need to operate. Dr. Langer is going to operate on you," he says. "The surgical resident will come and speak to you about it."

Later, as promised, the surgical resident comes in to see her. He tells her the same thing, that the massive therapy isn't working and that they are going to operate on her to close up the two wide-open ends and put new drains in. "We believe that will cure your infection," he explains.

She nods, but it's still all gibberish to her.

"Tomorrow," he says.

Tomorrow—that she understands. She is afraid and yearns for Cliff. She hangs onto the thought that he will be with her without fail at 7:00 PM. He strengthens her that evening.

"This is my third date with the knife," she jokes as she sees the surgical resident come in to prep her on the afternoon of October 21. "You ought to put a zipper in. It'd be much simpler to unzip me when you want to play with my innards."

He smiles and then swiftly injects her with atropine and methacholine at 4:00 PM. The plan is to keep her Intralipid, or subclavian, line open during surgery with 5 percent D/W. At 7:00 PM, another resident performs a coagulation screen for the OR—Langer does not want unstoppable bleeding to surprise him in the middle of surgery.

Meanwhile, the hospital calls Cliff at work. Cliff has a set route for his sales calls, and so it takes Viv in the office only ten minutes to track down his next client. She tells the client to have Cliff call TGH. She hangs up, swivels in her chair, and calls, "Girls …" The office staff soon all know that Judy is going under the knife again.

About thirty minutes later, Cliff has the news, too. He drives straight to TGH to wait in fear. His father has already made the funeral arrangements.

The orderly wheels Judy out of her room to her date with the scalpel as the sky blackens into night outside. At 7:45, she's in a small room with big, round lights staring down at her. She's surrounded by her surgical team: Langer, Chief Surgical Resident Dr. K. Wayne Johnston, their two surgical assistants, an anaesthetist, and the surgical nurses. They lift her off the gurney and onto a thin, hard surface. She feels like she is going to fall off. Her arms stick straight out to the left and to the right. She is on a surgical cross. Her heart pounds. They put a mask over her face and tell her to count backward. Her eyes close.

The anaesthetist suddenly calls out. Judy's blood pressure monitor reads zero; her pulse is non-existent. Judy lies lifeless on the table before them. They bag her quickly and pump air in and out of her lungs until the anaesthetist can slide a tube down her trachea and ventilate her with a machine. Meanwhile, a nurse hangs a unit of blood on Judy's IV pole and connects it to her line in an effort to increase her blood volume and thereby raise her blood pressure. Next, the nurse hangs a unit of packed blood cells. With no blood pressure, they cannot operate, and Judy will remain dead. They watch and wait. Her blood pressure rises, low but measurable. The team sighs in relief.

Langer incises her scar.

What the surgeons see is most bizarre. Although Langer had anticipated the mess revealed before their eyes, Johnston's eyes pop. Judy's duodenum is at one end, her large bowel stump at the other, both infected and scarred. The two ends have pulled apart, becoming unhealthy and ischemic, and are so far away from each other that it's impossible to reattach them. All they can do is oversew the bowel stumps with wire sutures and insert drains to siphon the congregating pus out of her abdomen. They thread a gastrostomy tube, or G-tube (a Foley catheter), through one of her fistula in the greater curve of her stomach and into the duodenum for decompression at 8:30. They use this tube as an air vent. Next, they cut more holes in her stomach to suction it independently through new drains. Finished, they sew her back up with wire sutures, as wire doesn't dissolve or react to skin, and they can easily remove them if they need to go in again.

The operation ends at 10:00 PM. Langer puts her alimentation on hold until the morning. The surgical residents take blood to measure her blood gases, and the GI (gastroenterology) residents take blood in the recovery room to measure her electrolytes, Hb, HCT, and WBC. Her post-operative orders include two milligrams of Talwin to be given as needed and 5 percent D/W to continue to keep her subclavian line open. Judy had received an inadequate three units of blood during the operation, and so the next day, they give her an additional four units of blood. In 1970, the risk of contracting hepatitis is low, and AIDS is not yet on the horizon. Receiving blood is worry free for Judy.

Langer finds Cliff in the waiting room and speaks to him quietly in a straightforward, matter-of-fact way. He explains that the operation went well but that Judy's chances of surviving and leaving hospital are small, both because she has severe peritonitis and internal fistulas from her duodenum and colon, and because there is no method that has been demonstrated to provide long-term nutrition outside of the hospital. After listening to Langer, Cliff continues to wait to see Judy when she comes out of the recovery room.

When he hears that she's back in her room, Jeej checks on her. Cliff is already there, sitting silently, looking worried.

"Will she live?" Cliff asks.

"We're doing everything we can. Dr. Langer has sewn up her bowels so they won't leak their contents into her peritoneum anymore. And the drains should drain out what bugs are left in there. This should cure her infection."

"She'll live?"

"I don't know. This is all experimental, you see. But we're hopeful."

The next day, fluid seeps through her dressings.

The following day, bloody and foul fluid runs out of her drains.

Chapter 8

Judy's Inspiration

The surgery has succeeded; the drains have cured her infection. The alimentation is strengthening her. And her hallucinations have stopped with the switch to methadone. Judy is emerging out of her semi-conscious haze. But Jeej is concerned. With Judy better able to understand the bleakness of her situation, death has a greater capacity to snatch her. Healing is not just a matter of treating the body, but also nourishing the soul. She needs to see why she's going through all this, he realizes. She needs to see her children. He explains to Cliff that seeing her children will boost her spirits and power her healing.

Back on Ivanhoe Court, Cliff has created a new routine for thirteen-year-old Cyndy, eleven-year-old Julie, and eight-year-old Miriam. He has asked his Aunt Connie, his father's sister, a woman he can lean on, to help him. She lives just south of Eglinton and Pharmacy, while they live near Lawrence and Pharmacy in Scarborough—a fifteen- to twenty-minute drive. Aunt Connie never had children, is single, and is a generation older than Cliff. Her notions about raising children come from a different era, and she is quiet like Cliff. But she is a willing spirit.

Aunt Connie arrives every morning to cook breakfast for the family. She sees the girls off to school and Cliff off to work. She gives them lunch, cooks dinner, puts the girls to bed, and goes home late after Cliff returns from the hospital. She runs the household, like Judy had, puts her focus on the children, like Judy had, and makes dinner the central family event with Cliff, herself, and the girls, like Judy had. She even makes rice or tapioca pudding every day as another measure of stability. And she tries to meet the girls' needs as their ages demand. Despite the fact that she argues with Cyndy over rules for thirteen-year-olds, she lets her stay up late to watch TV, unbeknownst to Cliff. One night, Cyndy is watching *Oklahoma!* when Aunt Connie suddenly scoots her off to bed. Cliff's headlights had just lit up the garage door. Julie, lying in her bed, hears the TV being switched off and Cyndy scrambling into bed. Julie isn't too happy with her older sister's special privileges. Why does Aunt Connie let Cyndy get away with stuff like coming home late from school and then getting to watch TV, she grumbles to herself. Why can Cyndy not accept what is told her, like she and Miriam do? But Miriam, lying awake in bed too, figures Cyndy, being much older, deserves special privileges, and when all goes quiet, she rolls over and cries herself to sleep, as she does every night.

No one speaks of Judy.

Cliff believes that the less said about her, the better for them. Neither Cliff nor Aunt Connie ever discusses Judy at the table or anywhere in front of the girls. They strive to create an atmosphere of normalcy, not wanting to alarm the girls. They believe they are sending the message that the girls' lives are about chores and homework, just like before, not about a dying mom.

Instead, their message creates unease and fear in the girls. To them, their mother has ceased to exist in the house on Ivanhoe Court, and their father appears only at dinnertime and then vanishes again. Living within this information vacuum, the girls learn to read moods. They know when something bad is happening to their mother because their dad becomes moody. Cyndy tries to eavesdrop to learn more.

She listens to the morning conversations between her dad and Aunt Connie when he relates what has happened the night before at the hospital. She listens to conversations between Aunt Connie and the neighbours as Aunt Connie brings them up to speed. She listens to her dad talk on the phone to their GP, Dr. Geoffrey Isaac, during his nightly calls. Still, in the end, she and her sisters only know that their mom is ill and that everyone's taking it day by day. That's it.

Then one Sunday morning, her dad announces that they will visit mom after the girls come back from church. The mother who has disappeared is suddenly reappearing in a new, unfamiliar setting.

It's a grey November day. Cliff piles the three girls in the car after they'd returned from church and eaten lunch and drives them and Aunt Connie down the Parkway to TGH. No one speaks. Fear of the unknown grips the girls. Hospitals are foreign to them. The only doctor they'd ever seen had been their GP in his office. All Cyndy can think about is that they are getting to see her because she has been classified as terminal. Their mom is going to die for sure.

They troop after Cliff into the pollution-blackened, red-brown brick building and along the brightly lit hallway, following the route Cliff has taken every day for almost two months now. It is quiet and empty until they pass through the right-hand jog, walk through a spot of partial darkness, and enter the brightly lit ward. They stop outside the nurses' station. The girls are scared. The smell is horrendous, a mixture of vomit and strong cleaning fluid. Cliff takes them in to the tiny room across from the station, and they see their mother for the first time since she had told them "I'll be back in an hour."

This is not their mother. She is bones. Her hair is lifeless, her skin dead. There are all sorts of things coming out of her and going into her. There is a pole beside her, bristling with bags and bottles, pushing fluid down a tube that disappears into her chest. She looks drugged. And the smell is worse.

Judy turns her head and smiles. Her face lights up, her arms reach out weakly, and the girls shuffle toward her. It is hard to hug her; they are afraid to hurt her. Miriam groans, puts her hand up to her mouth, and pukes before she can get to the bathroom. She doesn't even know where it is. An orderly quickly appears and swabs the floor. Cliff shows them the bathroom so that if one of the others throws up, she'll do it in the toilet. Only Julie is visibly happy to see her mother.

Judy tires quickly that first day, and Aunt Connie ushers the girls down to the cafeteria while Cliff stays with her. Judy is already snoozing. The cafeteria is in a burnt yellow-brown, subway-tiled basement. Glass doors mark the entrance to this utilitarian, windowless space. Aunt Connie sits with them as they nibble and wait for Judy to regain energy. This first visit sets the stage for every Sunday after. TGH becomes their second home; Sundays become a mindless routine of getting dressed, going to church, seeing Mom, taking turns puking, eating dinner in the cafeteria, and going to bed. Sometimes, surgery will prevent them from visiting, which upsets Julie greatly as she is always eager to see her mother again as soon as they leave. Sometimes, their Gammy joins them. Judy's mother keeps them company in the cafeteria, occupying their minds by asking about school and such things, while Cliff sits with a sleeping Judy. Miriam develops a fear of needles and tubes, and Cyndy blocks her emotions. Only Julie seems unaffected.

But now their dad appears, telling them that Mom is awake again and wants to see them. They straggle back up to her room for a second visit.

Judy brightens when they walk in. She feels so blessed to see them. She thrills to the touch of their small, warm hands touching her cold one. Their high-pitched voices fill her heart with love. Seeing them, she knows what she wants to live for. She will not accept death. Her body swells with determination to accept her situation so that she can live for these girls of hers. But too soon, fatigue washes over her, and she cannot resist it. She consoles herself with the knowledge that she will see them next week. She cannot wait. In any case, it's time for their dinner. She shoos Cliff off to the cafeteria with them.

Afterward, he drives his family, sans Judy, home in silence.

Chapter 9

The Langer Line

For the umpteenth time, the GI resident replaces Judy's plastic catheter. The residents have long since learnt to put in the plastic catheters and have taken over from the respirologists, but it's a job they'd rather not do so frequently. The alimentation is working well; Judy is reviving; it's time for her to receive a permanent catheter, one that is reliable and non-reactive—one that will last for years, won't fall out on a sneeze, and won't block easily. Langer thinks he knows what to use.

He'd heard about the catheters that the neurosurgeons were using to treat hydrocephalus. They'd developed tiny Silastic tubes that could be put into the brain, into the ventricles that contain cerebrospinal fluid, and then tunnelled down under the skin and either put inside the abdomen to drain the excess fluid there or put into a vein in the neck. The tubes can stay in the venous system for a long time. That's a fair distance to travel inside the body to shunt fluid from one end to the other, he thinks: if these silicone rubber catheters weren't inert and easy to fix into place, then there would be a bit of a problem brewing inside these patients. This kind of catheter is just what Judy needs. When Jeej tells Langer that the time is right to put a permanent catheter in, Langer heads down to the neurosurgery OR and retrieves a length of sterile catheter. He isn't sure of the exact length needed, but he knows from principle roughly how long it needs to be.

It's November 23, the day of Jeej's ninth anniversary, when he and his team prepare Judy for catheter emplacement. First, they X-ray her chest. All is fine. On the following day, Jeej and Johnston attempt to insert Langer's Silastic line into Judy's subclavian vein under a local anaesthetic in her room. But they're unsuccessful. They call the porter to transport Judy to the OR so that they can try again under sterile conditions and greater anaesthesia.

In the OR, Langer takes over from Jeej. He and Johnston attempt bilateral cephalic vein cut-downs, but they run into a small problem: Judy's cephalic vein is barely there. This attempt is also unsuccessful. The surgeons are disappointed.

Judy wonders about her future as the porter wheels her back to her room minus the permanent catheter that she'd expected. Later, Jeej explains to her the challenge they face and assures her that he and Langer are not going to give up.

He leaves to discuss this problem with Langer once again. They can't put in a permanent catheter without a vein strong enough to take it. And while they are on the subject, they talk again about how Judy will use it once she gets back home. They can't believe that they are actually discussing the daring possibility of managing her at home. This is virgin territory. They have no one else's experience to go on or to learn from. They finally decide on the facial vein as the point of entry into the jugular vein, which connects to the subclavian vein, the main entryway into the heart. The resident lets Judy know they're going to try again the next day.

November 25 dawns dreary. Rain distorts Judy's window, but fails to prevent her good friend Cathy Kelly from visiting her. Cathy's son had driven her down the previous day from her farm near Bobcaygeon, and Judy is thrilled to see her. Judy had resisted visits from her friends and neighbours at first, but now she thrives on seeing and talking with them. Cathy's visit breaks up the monotony of hospital life and distracts her from the wait, which in the end is not that long. The surgeons arrive. It's time for another attempt to put in her permanent line. As she is wheeled out, Judy waves and smiles at her friend, hiding her fear, protecting Cathy from worry.

Back in the OR, a room becoming all too familiar to Judy, the surgeons go into her mouth to incise her facial vein. The facial vein empties into the jugular, and, given their current technology, it's safer to insert the Silastic catheter into the facial vein rather than directly into the jugular. They thread it into the jugular and then the subclavian and down toward the heart. They stop when the tip reaches the atrium. Near this part of the heart, there's a huge amount of blood flow. With blood swishing by at such high volume and pressure, the chances of the line clotting on the end are much less. They wait while a radiologist X-rays her chest to confirm the tip is right where it should be.

One step done. Now, where to have the other end pop out? It cannot come out of her neck; it would be impossible for her to see and hook herself up to the alimentation. Instead, they tunnel it under her skin and bring it out the anterior chest wall, and there Langer decides to glue a small piece of Teflon to the catheter and then stitch the Teflon to the skin. The stitches will prevent it from migrating into her heart or disappearing underneath her skin, and gluing Teflon to the catheter allows the surgeons to anchor the catheter without having to tie stitches around it. Stitches could weaken or even penetrate the catheter itself over time. The newly dubbed "Langer Line" is finally in place.

Since they have her under anaesthesia and since her wound has healed so nicely, they also remove the wire sutures in her abdomen. She's sent to recovery and later to her room.

As she stares out the window at the rain, feeling the soreness of where her brand-new line was put in, she hopes Cathy can visit her again.

She does. The rainy, foggy weather continues into the next day. The dampness magnifies Judy's grogginess and post-operative soreness, but she perks up when she sees her friend walk through the door. Cathy shakes errant raindrops from her coat as she takes it off and drapes it over a chair. Judy doesn't notice the appalled look on her face as she gazes down on Judy before pulling a chair closer to the bedside and sitting down. Judy shifts her head so that she can see her friend better and ask how her trip went. Cathy inhales and exhales out her worry and responds to Judy's smile. Their cheerful chatter soon distracts Judy from her body and raises her spirits. The resident peeks in, sees Judy looking more relaxed, and cancels the STAT Valium he'd ordered just a few minutes earlier.

Chapter 10

Christmas

At my father's house, Jeej's house, all is still. I raise my head and listen to the dark. *Creak.* Shelagh, my black-lab mix, snorts and flops over. Silence. I creep out of bed, slowly raising the covers and trying not to make a sound. Last Christmas, Mummy and Daddy were furious at being woken up at "that ungodly hour." I tiptoe to the window and look outside. It's still dark, but isn't that just a hint of light way off through the trees there?

"Whatcha doing?"

"*Shhh.* Don't wake Mummy and Daddy up."

"I won't," says Pheroze, and he jumps out of bed. *Thud.* Right over their basement bedroom.

I roll my eyes. "Want to see what's in our stockings?" I don't tell Pheroze I'd stayed awake late enough to see if Santa Claus was really Mummy. I hug this new knowledge to myself.

"Yeah!"

We jump back onto our bunk beds, giggling and shushing each other, root around for our stockings, or rather the huge pillowcases buried under the blankets at the bottom of our beds, and eagerly dive into them. After the first squeals of delight and shushes, I slow down. I want to make it last, and breakfast is a long way off. We show each other what we got and play with the little toys. I'm hungry, so I eat my orange.

After what seems like hours, we crawl down the stairs, carefully open the basement door, tiptoe across to our parents' bedroom door, poke our heads around, and watch two sleeping heads.

"Are you awake?" we finally ask.

"*Hmmm?*"

Pheroze shoves past me and jumps on their bed. I hear an *oomph* and take that as permission to join him. We prattle on about what Santa Claus brought us, our narrative full of "and thens" until Mummy and Daddy sit up. Mummy lets us know it's not yet time for breakfast and orders us back to our rooms until she calls us. We groan. She relents and tells us we can play in the living room. "But quietly, and don't wake the baby." We thunder back upstairs to eye the Christmas tree with its hill of gifts underneath.

Meanwhile, across town, Judy's children are just waking up. Their father is the only parent in the house with them; they had hoped their mother would be back for Christmas, but she's still too sick. But that mound of gifts that had stood under the Christmas tree last night beckons them, and they stampede to the living room. They stop short. Their mouths open. No words come. The tree stands there, twinkling, decorated with baubles, bereft of the mound.

They hurry into the kitchen and ask their dad, "Where are the presents?"

"A burglar came and stole them all. There's no Christmas this year."

Miriam, eight-years-old like me, starts bawling. She cries out that he has to call the police.

"Did you call the police?" Cyndy asks.

"No. They're just cheap toys."

"You have to call the police. We gotta get our presents back!"

"Nah, you don't need them."

"Call the police."

"Yeah, Dad, call the police," Julie echoes Cyndy.

"All right, all right," Cliff says as he goes to the phone. He calls the police, or rather pretends to, tells the story, hangs up, and says, "Are you happy now?"

The morning drags on until lunchtime when Cliff says to them, "Now, hurry up and eat. We're going to go see your mom."

Their hearts sink. No Christmas? How will the police find them? Instead, they have to go to that yucky hospital. They flop down into their chairs and eat up. It doesn't matter what it is. It tastes like sawdust. Soon, they're finished and getting ready to visit their mom. They pile into the car and sit morosely in the back, the older two bugging their dad about their stolen presents, Miriam sniffling. He drives them down the Parkway to TGH and hurries them in, eager to stop the nattering.

"Come on, girls!" he demands as they shuffle their feet behind him. He pushes them into their mom's room. She sings out "Merry Christmas" as they each kiss her hello, but they cannot smile. It's just too awful, having no Christmas, and they tell her all about the burglar. As they're telling her their awful tale, they hear heavy footsteps behind them and turn to see their dad staggering in with suitcases. "Open them," he tells the girls. They do as they're told. Gifts spill out.

Their jaws drop. They look to their parents, who are grinning back at them like hyenas, and their eyes ask, "Can we?"

"Go on, open your presents," Judy says. Cliff sits down beside her and nods, too. The girls dive in. They tear at the gay wrappings and squeal over what they get. While they're occupied, Aunt Connie and Cliff's father and his wife enter, calling out "Merry Christmas!" They find seats and watch the girls' delight with Cliff and Judy.

The two tell them all about how they had decided to play a joke on the girls. They had thought it would be a hoot to have the girls think that someone had stolen Christmas and then bring them to see Judy and surprise them with all the Christmas glitter. Judy relates how on Christmas Eve after the children were in their warm beds, the sight of the tree twinkling promises of glee still in their heads, Cliff had packed up the gifts and stowed them in the car trunk.

Cliff picks up the story and regales them with how the kids had nattered at him all the way down to the hospital because he'd told them their presents had been stolen. "I said to them, 'It's only cheap toys. You don't need those. Well, it's lunch time. We'll go see your mom instead.' The looks they gave me." He rolls his eyes, and they rollick with laughter.

The girls interrupt to show off their gifts, being careful not to bump their mom in the process. Judy's heart bursts with such joy that she hardly notices the pain as they hug her. The horrors of the last few months fade.

Her doctor, my father, meanwhile, is enjoying this welcome day off, although he wishes he didn't have to be dragged out of bed quite so early. He heaves himself up and puts on his robe over his striped pyjamas. "Hurry up, Daddy," we encourage him. He picks up the pace and flops down on the chesterfield in the living room.

Mummy gets dressed because she has to make breakfast: waffles and bacon and lots of maple syrup. We're not allowed to open any of our gifts until we've eaten breakfast. Between bites, we crane our necks, trying to peek through the doorway into the living room of our bungalow, but she keeps us firmly in our seats until the last plate is licked clean. Finally given permission to excuse ourselves, we jump off our chairs to race to the tree. We bounce with impatience until she allows us to open one present each. Then we have to wait for Grandma and Grandpa and Uncle to show up. Finally, finally they're here. Everyone yells "Merry Christmas!" Grandma busses us on the cheeks, Uncle puts their gifts under the tree, and they all array themselves on the blue brocade chesterfield.

Mummy plays Santa Claus, handing out our gifts one at a time. We take turns opening them and watching what the others get. But it's over too soon, and she's back in the kitchen roasting a turkey, mashing potatoes, and boiling vegetables, while we play with our new presents until the scent of the cooking and our rumbling stomachs rev up the excitement again. The noise and happiness of the day keeps flowing into the night for us.

But for Cyndy, Julie, and Miriam, Christmas with both their parents is over. Judy is fading fast; she tries to ignore her creeping fatigue and the clouds gathering in her mind and the burning in her side. She tries to focus more intently on her children, on their joy and talk. But eventually, she has no choice but to succumb.

Cliff sees the blood draining from her face and her eyes drooping. He packs up the girls and gifts, and with good-bye kisses for her, they leave for the drive up north. Cliff is taking them up to the Kelly's farm to spend the holiday there. The farm sits next to the Taylors' cottage, and the girls will have a grand time playing in the snowy fields with the other kids, but Cliff will come back to the city to keep Judy company during Christmas week.

The rest of Judy's visitors leave shortly after Cliff and the children, saying they must get home before it gets too dark. Judy is alone.

The room is quiet. Judy looks around and hears the diminishing sounds of the girls' laughter and the tenor of Cliff's voice, sees the bright wrappings crushed in the garbage bin, and remembers the girls' pretty dresses. But the smell of hospital disinfectant and her own effluents, the squeak of nurses' shoes, and the greenness of the small room reassert themselves. It has been a good day. She falls asleep.

Chapter 11

Tests and More Tests

The air cracks outside with January cold. Inside the green walls of G South, doctors and nurses flood back from the Christmas holiday. Judy's room comes alive with voices, machines, and squeaking footsteps. Jeej enters for his morning rounds with the usual medley of residents and nurses in his wake. He brusquely tells her about his newest plan.

"We're going to do a liver biopsy on you," he says. He explains it and exits quickly with his entourage, on to see the next patient. He leaves Judy overwhelmed at the thought of having to undergo another painful procedure that she doesn't even fully understand. How much more pain will she have to endure? She picks up the carrots and celery on the plate in front of her. Jeej had prescribed them in order to keep her even white teeth in her jaw and to stop her gums from bleeding. She bites down hard on a carrot and chews and chews until only mush remains. She spits out the fibrous remnants and goes to sleep.

When Cliff arrives that night, she cries, "I'm not sure about it. I really don't want Jeej to cut me open again. I feel like a pincushion from all the needles, and my cheeks are black-and-blue from the vitamin injections. You just can't guess the pain from the sting of it going in."

"Well, Bones, Jeej must think it important for him to want to do it."

His nickname for her brings back her ready smile. He'd christened her "Bones" when she'd become emaciated, but for the last two months, she has been steadily putting on weight. Cliff takes her hand and says not to be afraid, that it isn't really cutting like surgery, but more like a poke. It will be okay, he assures her, and it will make her feel better. She's doubtful, but accepts it, as she knows it's for her own good. She blinks away her tears and asks after the girls. They're doing fine, he tells her.

The next morning, she tackles Jeej about this biopsy. He explains quickly, "Well, you know, fat is essential for good health. You need essential fatty acids because they're very critical in the building of the myelin sheath of the nerves so you can't omit it. But what we want to know is, is it causing you a fatty liver? The current feeling is that if you give fat, it'll make the liver fatty, and we don't want that. So, you see, we need to biopsy you to see what's going on. You see?"

Clear as mud, she thinks. But Jeej has brought her this far. She is alive. He won't let her die now. Besides, she has no choice.

When Pat comes in to check on her alimentation, Judy spills out her distress. The emotional roller coaster of anger, acceptance, fear is taking a toll. Pat asks if she wants to talk. She does. They talk about God, about prayer, and about faith.

"I pray all the time for Him to let me live," Judy confesses. "I tell him, Lord, don't take me, because he can't manage those three girls. I have to keep those girls together. Cliff can't do it."

"Sometimes, you know, God gives to us in mysterious ways. And, you know, we just have to have faith that he's going to see us through and carry on and live hour by hour and day by day. And hope for the best and pray for the best."

Judy nods and thinks about the biopsy planned for the next day. "You have to do what you have to do as long as it's going to help me in the end." She almost asks it as a question.

"Yes, it will help you. It will give Jeej more information about what is going on in you and if he is giving you the right stuff."

Judy nods again, lies back on her pillow, and closes her eyes.

On January 12, 1971, she undergoes her first liver biopsy. Afterward, Jeej tells her that he is very encouraged by the results. "Your liver showed mild, triadal inflammation, chronic pericholangitis, and occasional focal necrosis, but no fatty changes. This, after three weeks of starvation and then three months on alimentation with Intralipid."

Judy has no clue what he has just said, but if Jeej is happy and her liver isn't fatty, then she is happy, and she's just relieved it's over.

The procedures aren't over though, and her new G-tube continues to bother her. It is right at the bend in her hip, and it makes moving difficult. She has already begun a habit of placing her hand on her side to comfort it. When the residents ask her about it, she minimizes the pain. She absolutely doesn't want to go back on the morphine or to give them an excuse to keep her in longer.

In February, Jeej announces her next procedure in his usual rapid-fire speech, and, as usual, she barely understands. The bone marrow test goes well. In early March, Jeej tells her that he wants to do another liver biopsy. This time, she knows what to expect, but she doesn't understand why he wants to do another one.

Dianne Garde, the enterostomal therapist, whose job is to look after Judy's G-tube and teach her how to manage it, comes in to find her with tears flowing down her face. This is not the first time Dianne has found her crying after Jeej has left.

"I don't know what's going on. They're not telling me. He speaks so fast that I can't understand him, except he's going to do something painful. I can't keep up with him." Frustration chokes her silent.

"Look, you've got to tell him how you feel," Dianne says. "He's not God. He's a human being, you know."

Dianne looks straight into her eyes, and Judy sees the possibility that perhaps she can confront him. She wipes her face with the tissue Dianne hands her and takes a deep breath to release her tension. "I will speak to him," she says with determination.

The opportunity comes the next day during morning rounds. After examining her, Jeej turns to his students to discuss her impending biopsy. She interrupts his flow of instructions and informs him that she needs to understand what he is saying.

"I'll explain it to you later," he assures her.

She forces herself to insist that he come back after he finishes seeing the other patients, when he doesn't have his constant companions with him.

He chuckles and says he'll come.

And he does. She has it out with him. He listens intently. When she's done venting, he explains that he didn't know how she felt and that it's important that she understands what's going on; after all, she'll be in charge of her own care at home and will need to see her body and her health as he sees it. She'll need to understand all the terminology and how the alimentation and her G-tube work, and he assures her that he will not let her go until she feels secure about it all. She sighs with relief. She still looks upon him as God, fully believing he can do no wrong, but now she also sees him as her best pal. She realizes that this isn't being done to her anymore; she's a participant; he respects her as much as he respects his colleagues.

Judy excitedly tells Dianne later that night about the talk and how Jeej isn't so scary anymore. She can face this test and anything else he throws at her.

When he gets back the results of the biopsy, he shares his satisfaction with it with Judy and his residents. Although it has revealed triadal inflammation and fibrosis haemosiderosis, it shows no fatty changes. He is right—fat is good for her.

Chapter 12

Easter Tidings

Judy fishes the Gideon Bible out of her nightstand drawer. She holds it tightly in her two hands, eyes closed. Through her closed lids, she can feel the light of the sun shining through the uncurtained window. It is an unseasonably warm day. She opens her lids and looks at the title. She opens the cover, touches her name, which she'd inscribed there, and turns to the Gospel of John.

It's Good Friday. The day when God's painful plan for her Lord had unfolded. Jesus had pleaded with his Father to take the cup away, yet he submitted to God's plan willingly. Even as he hung on the cross, his weight slowly suffocating him to death, he thought of his mother, not his torment, and entrusted her to John's care. Judy finds comfort in that familiar story as she wonders about God's plan for her. She cannot see it yet.

She turns the thin pages to find her favourite passage. Romans 8:31–39 promises her that nothing will separate her from God's love—not her scarred body, not her pain, not her ill health, nothing. Just like God never forsook Jesus, He will never forsake her. She thinks again of that long-ago Friday. Although God's plan was for Jesus to die, He still mourned his death, darkening the skies, rumbling the earth, and rending the curtain in the temple. She feels death hovering near her. She prays again for God to take the cup away and to restore her life, for death not to be His will for her. She shuts the Bible and puts it back in the drawer.

On Easter Sunday, she rejoices in the chapel at Jesus's resurrection and prays for her own miracle. She holds that prayer in her mind as she wheels her pole back to her room, anticipating the girls' weekly visit. Her children arrive after church with Cliff and Aunt Connie. Her mother joins her later, and for a little while, she forgets about death and enjoys her family.

But Jeej has not forgotten. Even when he is not with his patients, he thinks about them, and over that weekend, he silently ticks off in his mind the risk factors for death that Judy has slowly but surely overcome: sepsis, jaundice, open belly, fistulae, and wide-open bowels. He suddenly realizes that she has beaten her infection and that his alimentation has restored to her a normal metabolism. She is likely to survive without too much difficulty. It is time to break this good news to Judy and Cliff.

Easter Monday, April 12, promises to be a warm, wet day. But Jeej hardly notices the drizzle as he strides along his usual route to TGH—he's thinking about the sweet news he's about to deliver. After depositing his doctor's bag and hanging up his coat in his office, he collects his entourage for morning rounds and visits Judy first, walking in smiling broadly.

He says, "I have been telling you that you're getting better. Well, I think now you will live. Your infection is under control, we are maintaining your metabolism, you're healing nicely, and you're looking good. I believe I can maintain you on central venous catheters and the alimentation. So you're going to live."

Judy's jaw drops. She snaps it shut and grins broadly. She is speechless for a moment. That night, she tells Cliff the good news. He's so relieved. His eyes fill up. No hope, no hope for so long. Now today, Easter Monday, there is hope.

Jeej pops in on his way home so that he can speak to Cliff, too. This is a moment to be savoured. Cliff asks him about taking Judy home. They are wondering which will be better: taking her home to Scarborough or to their cottage in Bobcaygeon.

"I think you need to prepare for the fact that you will be sitting around the house. You might be able to do a little bit of dusting, that sort of thing, but ..."

Judy breaks in. "Don't you think it would be more restful up in Bobcaygeon?"

"Well, possibly yes, if you're on a lake, that would be nice. You'll need a quiet life where you won't be disturbed too much," he answers.

Cliff isn't sure about going a hundred miles north of the city with three children and a wife who's on a contraption he still doesn't understand and has never seen before in his life. Only Jeej knows what this contraption is all about, and he'll be here, not up there. But Judy loves the cottage, and Jeej is saying she needs quiet, and Cliff is just happy that he's getting her back. Cliff agrees. Immediately, he starts thinking about winterizing the place and unpacking those rugs and panelling that he and Judy had picked out before she'd gotten sick.

In the next couple of months, he takes Cyndy up with him on weekends to the cottage. He lays the underfloor and carpets, puts the ceiling up, and finishes the walls and panels them while Cyndy assists. During the week, his neighbours continue the renovations. And every Monday night, he tells an eager Judy of their progress. They cannot wait for her to get home—home now being her favourite place, their cottage.

While winterizing the cottage, he thinks about finding a job. He'd been going out of his mind all this time with not knowing if Judy would live, and so he had taken a night course in oil burners. The evening of class was the only night during the week that he'd ever missed visiting Judy. The other nights, he'd brought his books with him to read when she was too tired to do much but say hello and sorry and fall asleep, only to wake up in time to say good-bye. That course will now stand him in good stead. He makes preparations to quit his sales job at Dominion Smallwares and to find a job as an oil-burner repairman up north. It will be a big cut in pay, but to have Judy back by his side is worth it. He will do anything for her. The funeral arrangements his dad made on his behalf are a distant nightmare.

Chapter 13

Going Home with Lester

"Well, now that you're going to survive, how do I get you off this damn IV pole?" Jeej says to Judy. She grins. He grins back and then concentrates on the problem. "Well, you don't eat over twenty-four hours," he says to the GI residents and nurses congregating around Judy's bed. "You only eat over a short period of time. So we have to take her off this pole and eventually get her down to just feeding at night."

They nod, all wondering how they will do this. They start thinking about how many calories she can absorb in a certain period of time without feeling nauseated, how they'll keep her line open with no solution constantly dripping into it, and how short they can make her alimentation time. At the moment, they're feeding her a day's worth of calories and nutrients 24/7, but that won't fly at home. She'll want to be free to move during the day, unencumbered by her IV pole. They have to cut her alimentation time in half, from twenty-four to twelve hours, so that she can start her alimentation before she goes to bed and finish it when she's ready to get up for the day. But first, they have to figure out how to disconnect her. Jeej puts his senior intern, Dr. John Wright, in charge of that first step.

Jeej turns back to Judy and tells her, "Now, while John is working on disconnecting you, you have to work on learning how to eat. You'll have to get used to being around other people while they're eating. Go down to the cafeteria with Cliff and have lunch with him."

Judy can't wait to tell Cliff this news. He beams when she does, and they set off. Judy looks like a Christmas tree in her flapping nightclothes, her pole festooned with bags and bottles, clanging and clunking, and her leg bag draped over her arm. The cafeteria staff hear them coming and stop them at the entrance.

"You're not allowed in here, ma'am."

"Dr. Jeejeebhoy sent us down. He told us to come for her to learn to be around other people when they're eating," Cliff replies.

"Doesn't matter. We can't have you upsetting the paying customers."

Cliff is mad; Judy is disgusted. They turn on their heels and clank back upstairs. Jeej pops in when he sees them disappearing into her room and asks them how it went.

"It didn't."

"Oh?" He raises his brows. His lips tighten as he listens to their story. He picks up the phone. "Cafeteria," he tells the operator brusquely. After a brief pause, he starts speaking. "Look, I sent my patient down to help her learn to be around people when they're eating. She needs to get used to this, and you need to understand that this is a teaching hospital, and this is life. And you'd better get used to it. Uh-huh. Uh-huh. Well, if you lose some sales, that's too damn bad. I don't want to hear about you stopping her again. Uh-huh. Well, the cafeteria is for the patients. It's not for anybody else. You better get used to it, understand? I'm sending her back down." He waits to hear compliance before hanging up.

"You can go back down. I've sorted it out."

They go back down. The staff again hear their clangour before seeing them but let them in this time. Their eyes follow the couple as Cliff seats Judy before he goes over to the counter to get a hot meal. The patrons, too, stare at Judy. They don't even cease staring when Cliff returns to the table and glares back at them, for Judy is sitting there with no food in front of her, just watching Cliff eat. There's a hunger in her eyes as she follows his fork as it scoops up the food and moves it to his mouth and back down to his plate.

Suddenly, she snitches a morsel of food from his plate and chews it, savouring the flavour and texture until it is reduced to tasteless mush. Joy lights up her face and obliterates the disgust she feels at the cafeteria staff. She spits it out discreetly into a napkin. She smirks at Cliff for her naughty behaviour. She can't wait to do it again. Meanwhile, it's back to bed.

Wright follows them back into her room and sends Cliff out into the hall. He thinks he knows how to disconnect her from her alimentation while keeping her subclavian line open. Cliff, standing near the nurses' station, watches Wright coming out of her room, going back in, leaving the room, going back in as he attempts this feat two or three times. On one of his trips past Cliff, he pauses to explain that he's trying to decide how much heparin to put in the line to keep it from clotting. It's a bit of a struggle, he admits. Finally, he comes out for the last time, relief relaxing his face.

"You can go in now," he tells Cliff. "I'd like it if you could take her for a short walk down the hall; then we'll reconnect her." He leaves for a few minutes of decompression.

Cliff goes into the room and assists Judy out of bed. She wobbles and grabs Cliff's arm. For over six months, she has not stood on her own—she's had her pole to lean on. They shuffle out of the room and down the hall a short way, then back again. Judy gets into bed with great relief, her legs shaking with fatigue. Wright returns replenished, ready for the next big step—hooking her back up.

The next morning, Jeej asks Judy how it went and is pleased with the success of the disconnection.

"Good," he says. He begins to interrogate his residents about the next phase of her recovery: reducing the time she is on her alimentation. Some of his students offer various possibilities before realizing that the pumps currently in existence cannot pump 300 cc per hour, the rate to which they need to increase the infusion. The Intralipid easily drains into her line under the force of gravity, but the Amigen-dextrose mixture comes in bags and needs to be pumped in. Noticing blank faces, Jeej suggests using air pressure, and he puts Wright onto developing a pressurized system.

"Let's start with reducing her alimentation time to twenty hours," he instructs Wright before leading them all out to see the next patient.

Over the weekend, Wright finds three 1,000 cc blood pressure cuffs. He commandeers a pressurized air tank. He gathers up some tubing and clamps. With all these pieces, he engineers a new system for Judy on her very own IV pole.

He enrobes the Amigen-dextrose bags in the blood pressure cuffs. He hooks the bags up to each other with tubing and the cuffs to each other with their own tubing. He connects the end cuff to the air pressure tank and turns on the tank. He had calculated the required pressure beforehand and watches the dial creep up to his target number. He switches off the tank. The cuffs have all swelled. He flushes Judy's line and connects the nearest bag's tubing to it. The last bag on the line starts emptying as the alimentation flows from one bag into the next and finally into Judy under pressure of the cuffs. As that bag empties, its cuff deflates, and the next bag starts emptying. Wright sets a timer to monitor the rate of flow and to ensure that this first incarnation finishes in twenty hours, as Jeej wants. As he tells Pat on Monday, "She can just go to bed and not have to wake up to change the bags."

Emboldened by the knowledge that she will live, Judy takes back some control over her destiny. She asks the nurse for writing paper and pulls the bed tray close. She writes, "Room 1346—G West, College Wing T.G.H., May 18, 1971." With the proper addressing done, she gets down to business. With a fine-tipped pen and in her neat, right-leaning cursive with nary a printed letter and all the capitals done as elementary-school students are taught, she writes:

Dear Dr. Fenton

I feel the time has come to put into written form my request for information re my equipment. First of all I would like you to know we do appreciate your interest in my case and the trouble you have taken in looking into safer, more practical equipment for me to take home. I understand this equipment has now been decided upon but has not been ordered yet.

She continues on a new page, her writing sloping more, thinning the letters:

Could you please be good enough to explain to me why this order is being held up and how long I can expect to wait? My family is moving as of the second week in June and I must make some plans between now and then.

Realizing that you will understand how I feel in this matter. I am sure I can expect a reply in the next few days.

Thank you again for your interest and kindness.

Yours truly

Judy Taylor

She has one more letter to write, even though her hand is cramping up. She addresses it properly before writing:

Dear Dr. Jeejeebhoy;

We know there is no way in which we can thank you and Drs. Langer and Johnson for what you have done for me but "thank you" anyway. Enclosed please find a letter (copy) of a request I am sending to Dr. Fenton re my equipment.

With our most grateful thanks I remain

Yours truly

Judy Taylor

Later that month, the staff members decorate an IV pole with a big red bow, and one of Judy's favourite residents, Dr. John Zohrab, nicknames it "Lester." The nurses and residents wheel "him" in together, laughing and smiling as they officially present Lester to Judy. She guffaws at her new friend and quickly receives him. She loves Lester; for as long as he is with her, she is not dead.

She cannot wait to care for her family again. She soaks up everything the nurses teach her about the technology. Cliff, too, does not fear the responsibility that is to come; he's focused only on getting his wife back. The staff teach them how to set up the apparatus and how to clean her skin and her line. They teach Judy how to hook herself up and how to maintain her G-tube. They drill into both of them the danger of infection—she cannot afford to even get a cold—and that a temperature, even a mild one, means danger. She must immediately come down to TGH, they assert. She confides in Pat her concerns about social issues and being intimate with Cliff because of her abdomen being criss-crossed with scars and tubes coming out of her. Pat reassures her, but no one anticipates that soon after returning home Judy and Cliff will discover that intimacy is out of the question. Her body is too fragile and sunken to make it possible. He remains monogamous and committed to her, even though she confides to a friend years later that she wouldn't have minded if he'd had an affair. For herself, she didn't miss it. She was alive, everything else came second, and if that was the price to pay for living, then so be it.

Worried about the long drive from Bobcaygeon to Toronto, Jeej has the residents arrange for a plane to be available from CFB Trenton for swift transport. Zohrab gives them written instructions on how to contact the base in the event of an infection or line blockage.

The last thing for Judy to learn is how to walk on her own again without leaning on Lester or Cliff. For each month in hospital, it takes a month to recover. She's been visiting fellow patients all up and down the ward, sometimes with Lester, sometimes without, gabbing and offering sympathy, devising practical jokes to play on the residents with like-minded friends. Now, she's sent outside on short excursions to Eaton's department store, just down the street at College and Bay. She thrills to being outside, being part of normal life again. Things are looking up; she can see the light at the end of this long tunnel.

Unexpectedly, Jeej orders the Intralipid stopped. "Your serum triglycerides have risen," he explains. "We're going to replace the lost calories with dextrose." Over the next several days, he comes in on his morning rounds looking worried. Cliff asks him what the problem is.

"I don't know," Jeej replies. That is all he says.

At first, they cannot understand. He is the doctor. Why doesn't he know? Well, Cliff points out to Judy, at least he is honest.

Finally, Jeej knows the answer, courtesy of his neighbour and colleague, Dr. Brian Webster. "It's your thyroid," he declares.

"My thyroid?" Judy replies.

"It has become underactive."

"Oh, I'd forgotten all about that!" Judy exclaims, and she tells him about how it had been irradiated and about how she'd gone on these pills. It had seemed so long ago and irrelevant, and she'd been so sick that neither she nor Cliff had thought to tell Jeej.

"No matter," he assures her. "But we can't give you pills now. They'll go nowhere in you. We're going to have to come up with an IV form of l-thyroxine. I've discussed it with Baun. He'll create it for you."

The new medicine does the trick, as Jeej would say, but he decides against putting her back on the Intralipid. He sees this situation as a unique opportunity to observe what will happen when she's not receiving any fat, to compare the effects of fat versus carbohydrates on the liver. Around the same time, he receives the pathology report dated June 16 on sections of Judy's excised mesentery, gall bladder, jejunum, ileum, and colon. The pathologist found many areas of full-thickness necrosis and gangrene, acute purulent exudates on the peritoneum, and a very large number of thrombi in the intramural, particularly in the submucosal veins of the intestine, and also in the mesenteric vein. The arteries were normal. In other words, clots had formed in the major vein that drains the bowels, stopping the blood from flowing out of this organ and back to the lungs for oxygenation. Since blood could not flow out, it also could not flow in to oxygenate the cells. The clots had starved her intestines of nutrients. They died. Jeej hypothesizes that the birth control pill, which is known to increase the risk of clot formation, is the cause of all these thrombi, particularly since Judy had started on a high dose of two milligrams, later reduced to one milligram in February 1967 after she developed a pregnancy mask. Judy is now off the birth control pill.

At last, the big day arrives. Sunday, July 11, 1971. Cliff carries a mountain of supplies to his car while Judy waits for him in her room. She is dressed, and she is excited. All day, nurses, residents, and patients have poured in, wishing her goodbye, a safe journey, and good luck in her new life. Jeej comes in smiling broadly. She smiles back. At last, Cliff walks in and holds out one arm to her. She takes it. They leave her room together; they leave the ward together; they leave College Wing together; they walk into the parking lot and toward their car together. Cliff opens the passenger door for her. Judy climbs in, smiling. He shuts it. He walks around to his side, opens his door, starts the car, and drives out of the lot toward home. He, too, is smiling.

Chapter 14

A Different Kind of Dinnertime

Judy loves to cook. It is her favourite way to minister and nurture her family. She has had to sublimate this desire for ten months while she learned a new way of preparing her own nourishment and "eating." Now, finally, those months are over. She is cooking for her family again. Even though she is weak from those months in hospital, she doesn't wait to re-establish her family dinner and family shopping rituals. These are the best expressions of her life's purpose.

The genesis for the week's meals happens on Thursdays. Her shopping list is easy to draw up, for each night of the week has its designated meats, from sausages on Mondays to hot dogs on Fridays and her handmade hamburgers on Saturdays, her so-called night off. Once she hears the car crunch up the driveway, she and the girls pile in, and Cliff turns it around to drive to Lindsay for grocery shopping.

Cliff and the girls stay in the car, watching for Judy through the windows as she wheels the shopping cart up and down the aisles of the Lindsay supermarket. When she approaches the cashier, he goes into the store to pay for the groceries with cash and loads them up in the car while Judy goes to sit in the front passenger seat.

Back at home, the family puts away the groceries before sitting down to dinner. Afterward, Judy feeds herself while Cyndy watches—but does not touch or handle any of the supplies or equipment—and Cliff assists. This is technical stuff. There is no joy in injecting vitamins into IV bags and plugging those bags into catheters. For Judy, the joy comes in the tactility of raw food, the aromas of cooking food, the stolen tastes of food prepared by her hands. Sundays especially are her domain—she will have it no other way—and Sundays mean a big roast beef.

Before church, Judy removes the large roast from the freezer to thaw. After lunch, she shoos the family away so that she can cook dinner. Alone in her kitchen, she hefts the bound roast into her trusty pan, the firm meat giving under her hands. She spices it with salt and pepper and cozies cut onions around it. She turns the oven on and slides the pan onto the upper rack. As the beef roasts, she pulls the potatoes one by one out of their dark bag. Their hardness is no match to her expert skinning of their thick peels, which pile up quickly in the sink. She boils the potatoes on the stove. Out of the freezer, she takes a bag of mixed frozen vegetables and boils those, too, just before serving.

At her command, Cliff switches off the TV, and they all sit down at the table, including Aunt Connie, who has just arrived from her new home in Bobcaygeon. Cliff carves and serves the roast onto five plates. Judy heaps the vegetables and potatoes beside the tender slices and passes the plates to the others. Her heart is full as she serves her family the meat and fruits of her love and sees the girls' eyes widening with anticipation.

Judy places no plate in front of herself. Instead, she puts a clear glass of water at her right hand. She sips it occasionally as she chats with her family, her big voice and big laugh filling the room and her warm eyes drawing her children, Cliff, and his aunt to her and their stories out of them. Their knives and forks clink against their plates, slicing meat and forking up the soft mashed potatoes, chasing errant peas, trying not to see Judy with only a glass of water in hand.

That water glass screams: "Why isn't Mom eating dinner?" The silent question goes unanswered at the dinner table. As the girls tell of their escapades, another question lurks deeper in their hearts: "What will happen to her and to them?" They watch Judy place her water glass down, her laughter joining their giggles.

Cliff and Aunt Connie eat while the girls exclaim, "Great meal, Mom!" But Cliff's guilt silences him. How can he extol the succulence of her roast beef, the butteriness of her mashed potatoes, or the sweet crunch of her famous cookies when his praises serve only to salivate her appetite, an appetite that if satiated would kill her? But Judy knows only gratitude to once again be sharing a meal with her family in their new home by the lake, each person in his or her place. Besides, Judy's appetite, gnawing at her stomach, had already driven her to sip the thin brown juices from the roast pan, to savour the texture of the melten beef fat on her tongue, to chew a morsel of the tender cooked meat before spitting it out into a napkin. She's careful not to do the latter in front of Miriam, who'll screw up her face and yell, "Oh gross, Mom!"

Dinner finished, Cliff announces to the kids, "Time to wash up." The girls rotate chores. Tonight, Miriam and Julie clear the table and wash the dishes in the kitchen, while Cyndy scrubs the plastic tablecloth covering their imitation-mahogany dining table to ready it for assembling Judy's alimentation. Cliff goes to the second fridge out on the porch to retrieve Judy's alimentation supplies. He removes three one-litre bags of Amigen-dextrose containing Amigen, dextrose, sodium chloride, sodium lactate, calcium gluconate, potassium chloride, magnesium sulphate, and trace amounts of zinc, cobalt, manganese, copper, and iodine. He deposits these on the table, being careful to keep their exit tubes off the table-top, so they can warm up. Judy had quickly learned how uncomfortably cold the alimentation is when going into her veins straight out of the fridge.

They wait to start her feeding until after the younger two have gone to bed and Aunt Connie has left. While Cyndy chats at the table with Judy, Cliff goes to the second fridge and comes back with an ampoule of MVI and a bottle of heparin. He places those on the table, again being careful to keep their ends off the surface. Next, from the back room, he retrieves medication injection sites, a bottle of 80 percent isopropanol, pre-filter sets, a final bacterial filter set, Garamycin cream, Detergicide, and a plasma transfer set plus a box of gauze, non-allergenic adhesive tape, plastic syringes and disposable needles, and tubing sets and a veno-tube. He leaves the sterile gloves on the shelf.

Judy flips through the pages of the final summary that Zohrab had given her until she finds the list of supplies and double-checks what is on the menu today. Yesterday, she'd pencilled in the margins that she'd taken the Synkavite, folic acid, Synthroid (her thyroxine replacement), and rubramine, and Cliff has the cut on his finger from breaking off the ampoule tops to prove it. His fingers are clumsier than Judy's.

Before beginning, they wash their hands with soap and water. They don't use masks and no longer use the inconvenient sterile gloves since Jeej had taught them the no-touch method. This method requires they not touch any part of the supplies that will go into a tube, a bag, or Judy; in that way, they prevent infection.

While Cyndy sits and watches, Judy unwraps a syringe and then one of the disposable needles, being careful not to touch its tip. She puts the needle in the syringe and props it up so that the needle is off the table. Using a serrated knife, she scores the glass ampoule and breaks the top off. She doesn't cut her finger. She picks up the syringe and sucks out 5 cc of MVI. Cyndy asks her what it is. Judy answers it's her vitamins. Cyndy asks why she needs them. Judy answers that the doctors want her to take them. Cyndy asks her what they're for and what's in the bags. Judy continues to answer all her questions as patiently and as simply as possible.

Cyndy strains to comprehend what Judy is saying, but it's years before she fully understands that without all this stuff, her mother would die.

Meanwhile, Cliff unwraps an injection site and tubing, being careful not to touch the ends of the tubing, picks up a bag of Amigen-dextrose, puts the injection site into it, and then puts the tubing into the injection site. Judy hands him the syringe of MVI, and he shoots it into the bag. He connects the three bags with tubing and attaches the filters into the end tubing and the venotube, its free end covered with a blue plastic protector. He places the bags inside the blood pressure cuffs, which are already attached to the pressure gauge on the air tank clamped onto Lester. He slowly opens the valve and raises the pressure to 200 mm Hg. He switches off the tank. He squeezes the last bag so that the solution runs down the tubing and through the filter sets, pushing all the air out. He clamps the end of the tube.

Judy removes the sterile dressing that covers her Langer Line and the heparin-filled syringe attached to it. It's a bit hard for her to see it, and she has to stretch her neck and tuck her chin in. She opens a package containing a cotton wipe and soaks the wipe with Detergicide. She wipes off all the encrusted material on her skin and around the line. She removes the syringe from her line and plugs the end of Amigen tubing into it. She unclamps the tubing, and the solution slowly drips in while they watch, Cliff sick with fear of it clotting and stopping the flow—which would mean a fast trip down to TGH and Jeej. It would also mean that Judy could die. His heart pounds with each drop that flows down the tubing and into Judy. She just watches. Finally satisfied that all is well, Judy sends Cyndy off to bed and retires to her chair to knit and watch TV for a couple of hours. Cliff follows her and sits in his chair. The alimentation ritual has taken fifteen minutes.

Chapter 15

Supply Run

The initial mountain of supplies and solutions has vanished. It's time for the supply run. They had received two weeks worth of alimentation, for the solutions last only so long, even in the refrigerator. It's just as well; it's good for Judy to stop by Jeej's office so he can see how she's doing. How she looks tells him much about how well she's maintaining herself.

Cliff takes care of the supply-run preparations—the ordering, the loading, and the unloading—to ease the burden on Judy. Besides, she doesn't have the energy or muscle strength to do it.

Before the initial run, he builds a trailer to carry the Everest of supplies: tubing, solutions, bandages, bottles, the occasional air tank, syringes, disposable needles, her alimentation, and assorted vitamins and medications. He puts a thermos cooler in the trailer to keep the solutions cool on the drive home and hooks the trailer up to the car hitch.

"Judy," he calls out. She emerges from the house with tins of cookies: a special one for Jeej, one for the nurses, and one for Cliff to give to the pharmacy technicians. He opens the car door for her, and she climbs in. He gets in the driver's seat, pulls the choke, and starts the ignition. They're off. They drive down Highway 35 through Lindsay to Highway 401. He merges into the traffic of long cars and big trucks and flows with it toward Toronto and the Don Valley Parkway. The Parkway is familiar territory. Memories of driving down it night after night flood Cliff as he comes round the curve off Highway 401 and sidles right into the Parkway traffic. He glances at Judy next to him and then back at the road. Soon, he is pulling up to the College Street entrance to TGH and letting her out to visit Jeej and the ward. He then wheels the car round to the service entrance off of Elizabeth Street.

It's a bit of a bitch manoeuvring the trailer into the loading-dock area. The place is filled with trucks loading and unloading, driving in and out. The trailer is unwieldy. After forwarding and reversing futilely for a while, he gets out, unhitches the trailer, and manhandles it to the loading dock. He slams back into the car and reverses it up to the trailer. He hooks it back up. He walks into Pharmacy, where the pharmacy tech is waiting for him.

"Hi, Cliff," he calls out. "I have some of your supplies ready on this cart. I was just waiting for you to come before taking the cold items out from the fridge."

"Sure," Cliff replies. "Here, she made these for you." He hands over the tin of cookies. The tech takes the tin, opens it, and peeks inside. A smile engulfs his face.

"Thank you! I'll take these in back to share with the others."

Cliff follows him and finds George Tsallas, a pharmacy student working with Baun (he later takes over when Baun leaves). George quickly puts down his work when he sees Cliff and starts chatting with him about how the first two weeks back at home went. The weeks have passed uneventfully, he tells George, but his smile says that he's still walking on air from having Judy home. She's cooking dinner, doing a bit of vacuuming, and looking after him and the girls, Cliff continues. She likes to sit outside by the lake and read. He has to keep the girls from worrying their mother—you know what kids are like—and he's getting into his new job as an oil-burner repairman. Judy isn't having any problems with her solutions, but that darn G-tube still irritates her. Nothing she can't handle, he finishes up. George listens fascinated, not only by how she's doing on the alimentation at home on her own, but also with their life up in Bobcaygeon.

The pharmacy tech interrupts them to say he's ready to wheel the carts out to Cliff's trailer. "Just a minute," George tells Cliff as he's about to say good-bye. He grabs some forms and hands them to Cliff, telling him to fill them in and mail them before coming down. That way, they can ensure that all the supplies are ready to go. Today, there are no changes in the alimentation, but in the future, George will explain any new changes to Cliff so that he can then instruct Judy. Cliff and George say good-bye.

While Cliff is in Pharmacy, Judy is making her way to Jeej's office. She smiles hello to his secretary and asks if he's in. She sits down to wait. Before long, Jeej comes out with a patient and sees Judy, and a great big smile comes over his face.

"Hello!"

"Hi, Jeej. These are for you," Judy says as she hands him his tin.

"For me? What's in here?"

"Open it!"

He peels the lid up toward him and peeks over it into the tin to see a pile of chocolate chip cookies staring back at him. "Oh, wow!" He takes one and bites into it. "These are good," he compliments her through a mouthful of crumbs.

She grins. He swallows and reaches in for another, but before he bites it, he asks, "So how are you doing?" He really looks at her as he listens to her airy "Fine, never felt better Jeej," noting her skin tone, her hair condition, the way she's holding herself, her eyes. These features tell him what she's telling him, that she feels well. Even though she does not have that attractiveness of good health, the kind that infuses the face with energy and lets the body stand loose, her spirit oozes warmth and joy to such an extent that it pulls people to her and blinds them to the weakened body it resides in. People rarely want to stop talking to her; Jeej doesn't want to stop talking, but he has a patient waiting.

Judy waves good-bye to Jeej and heads to G South.

"Hi, Judy!" Pat calls out and comes out of the nurses' station. She's thrilled to see Judy looking so good and obviously enjoying being back home. The cookies are a welcome sight, too. The tin goes on the counter, the lid comes off, and nurses help themselves as they stop to talk to her.

"Jeej told me to visit ..." She pauses as she searches for the name.

Pat knows the name. She and Jeej had discussed having Judy visit their newest patient on alimentation. Now that Judy has shown long-term alimentation to be not only feasible but successful, Jeej can use it on other very sick patients. But most are having a harder time adapting than Judy had, and Pat and Jeej believe that if these patients can see someone who is enjoying life and looking vibrant while on alimentation, then that will give them courage to accept this new way of eating.

Pat walks with Judy to the patient's room and leaves the two women alone. Judy sits down, introduces herself, and explains how easy her alimentation is and what a lifeline it is. "It only takes me fifteen minutes every night," she assures this patient. "I feel great. Look how good I look too!"

The patient isn't convinced.

"It doesn't have to be a big deal. It isn't as if you will be stuck in bed and feeling sick all the time. You'll feel great, I promise you."

"What about eating?"

"You'll never get over eating. You will always want to eat something. You will have to work to get over it. You just go through it one day at a time."

"That's not encouraging."

"I can just tell you to accept it and get on with your life."

The compassion emanating from Judy's eyes, the warmth of her spirit, and the strength of her heart sink into the woman lying in bed. Slowly, slowly, as she looks up into Judy's smiling face, she realizes that maybe this alimentation thing will be okay.

She is the first of many whom Judy will visit in the coming years, visits she'll enjoy making on every supply run as a way to help the team that helped her. She says good-bye and heads back down the hall to the nurses' station. Though she does not want to admit it, she's tired.

As Judy is walking down the hall, Cliff is towing the full trailer out of the loading area in search of a two-car parking spot. There aren't many legal ones, and he quickly parks in the first one he finds. He walks into College Wing, knowing where to find Judy. She'll be with the nurses or one of the patients. When she was still in hospital and had become ambulatory, she hadn't stayed in her room much if she could help it. She had made many friends and preferred visiting them in their rooms, whether to team up with one to play practical jokes on the residents or to cheer another who was going through a difficult procedure. Judy, Cliff thinks, likes to help people. It's just one of the many reasons he loves her.

He finds her chatting to Pat about the patient she'd just talked to. He notices her pale face and says nothing. She wouldn't want him to. She gathers up the empty tin from the counter, and they walk out to the car for the return journey home.

Back in Bobcaygeon about 5:00 PM, Judy carries the tins into the house, washes up, and lies down on the couch for a brief nap before starting dinner. Cliff unloads the trailer. He puts the solutions and vitamins into the second fridge and brings the rest of the supplies into the back room. He unhooks the trailer and pushes it out of the way. He then follows Judy into the house to read the paper until dinner is ready.

Chapter 16

Essential Fat

It's almost time to leave for school, and Cliff has told the girls that they are not to wake Judy up. But Miriam lingers outside her parents' bedroom, watching her mother's closed eyes, watching for a sign that she can talk to her. She hadn't wanted her mom to come home from the hospital. It had been too long, and she'd feared that her mom would smell like the hospital, have tubes, and may not be normal. But now, she yearns to talk to her mom every morning. Unfortunately for her daughters, Judy usually sleeps in until after they all leave for the day, until her alimentation has almost run out. Miriam looks over her shoulder to make sure her dad doesn't see her. She returns her gaze to her mother's eyes, searching for the slightest flicker. Judy rolls over and flips her eyes open. Miriam races in. She chatters to her mom until it's time to leave for school. Outside the bedroom door, she bumps into her dad, who is none too happy about Miriam waking her mother up. Judy calls out from the bed that it's okay, that she was awake, and Miriam dashes off to school on this cold, early-January day.

It's the weekend. Today, Miriam doesn't have to sneak a morning visit; she can wait to see Judy. Everyone goes outside to play, and Judy gets some peace for her last hour of sleep.

Judy's eyes snap open. She looks at Lester. The last bag is almost empty, but she has a moment to enjoy this last little bit of rest. She turns her head to look out the window. I could be pushing up daisies, she thinks as she gazes on the falling snow outside her window. I have lived one more day. I have an extra day to see Cliff, Cyndy, Julie, and Miriam. Her entrancing smile lights her face at the thought, and she gets up to prepare her dressing tray. But first she trundles to the bathroom.

She wheels Lester to the kitchen and opens the tap over a large roasting pan. She carries the pan to the stovetop and places a metal dressing tray and forceps in the water. She turns the electric burner on and waits until the water in the pan has boiled for fifteen minutes. When the water has cooled, she fetches her supplies, takes the tray out of the water, and places the supplies along with the forceps onto the tray and carries it to the bathroom counter.

Standing in front of the mirror, she clamps the tubing shut. She carefully peels off the gauze taped over the catheter site and tosses it in the garbage. She rips open a cotton-wipe package, unscrews the cap of the 1:750 Detergicide solution, upends the bottle over the wipe, and gently cleans off all the dried pus around the catheter site. She shuts out of her mind the rawness of her skin. She chucks the wipe in the garbage and, before picking up the Garamycin cream, idly scratches her arm. She squeezes some cream onto her fingers and strokes it around the catheter site. It brings relief.

She takes a 10 cc plastic syringe out of its package and a 22-gauge disposable needle out of its package. She inserts the needle into the syringe and plunges that into a bottle of heparin, sucking up 10 cc. She places the syringe, needle up, on the tray and scratches her other arm.

She clamps her line, unplugs the alimentation, picks up the syringe, removes the needle (tossing it into the garbage), and attaches the syringe to her line. She unclamps the line, pushes the syringe's plunger until 7 cc of heparin have disappeared down her line, reclamps, rips off a piece of tape from the roll sitting on the tray, tapes the plunger to the syringe, rips off another piece of tape, and tapes the syringe to her skin. She then opens a package of gauze and tapes a square of it over the entire site.

She scratches her first arm again and repeats the cleansing procedure on her G-tube site. Her flank burns, and she steels herself before wiping it clean. She dollops on generous amounts of soothing Garamycin cream as tears stain her cheeks with salt. She retapes the tube onto her skin, hopefully in a position that will not pull too much as she moves. She rips open a sterile dressing and tapes that over the G-tube. She detaches the straight drainage tubing and disposable urine-collection bag from the free end of the G-tube. She disposes of the bag and puts the tubing over the side of the tub for the moment. Her bile bag has been drying overnight there, and she picks it up, attaches it to her G-tube, and straps it to her leg. She had put a few drops of deodorant in it the night before, which will neutralize the smell of her stomach fluids as they drip into the bag during the course of her day. She sniffs the air, but detects no smell.

She removes the empty Amigen bags out of their cuffs and throws them into the garbage along with all the empty packages and used disposable supplies. She scratches her leg, realizing this time what she's doing and tries to stop herself. Her skin everywhere is cracked, the cells splitting apart, their edges peeling up until her scratching dislodges them in flakes. Moisturizer is no help. Although she accepts her skin plaguing her as another part of being the first person on alimentation, the past two or three months have been uncomfortable. On her last supply run, Jeej had taken blood from her, which he had sent to the Banting Institute for special testing. Apparently, the results are in, and Jeej wants to see her.

Pushing Lester in front of her, she exits the bathroom, walks down the hall, pushes him into his closet, puts on a kettle to boil, and looks out the living room window as she waits. You're a lucky girl to be able to do that, she thinks.

The kettle whistles. She carries it to the bathroom, pours it through the straight drainage tubing along with some Detergicide, and leaves it to dry over the side of the bathtub. All that's left is to get dressed. Today, she's going to TGH for some tests. Jeej orders these and other tests after much thought on his part, but with little notice to her and Cliff, in order to assess her nutritional status and/or to figure out the cause of puzzling problems. Yet as scary as these tests are to her, they have become a frequent part of her life, and she plays them down to all and sundry; she especially characterizes them to her girls as routine and just a normal part of life. She doesn't want them to feel the fear that she does.

Cliff has already put her suitcase in the car and is ready to drive through the snow-piled streets for what Judy and Cliff characterize to their daughters as a routine trip to TGH for some tests. Outside, she kisses the girls good-bye and tells them that Mrs. Kelly will get them dinner. They wave good-bye before scampering off to play. They don't start worrying until she doesn't come home that night.

Back on G South, they biopsy Judy's liver. It's January 3, 1972. The results are sent to Jeej fairly quickly. He scans them, realizes what he must do, and heads to the ward to tell Judy.

He sits down by her bed, crosses his arms, leans back in his chair, and launches into an explanation of his plan for her. Her smile never wavers.

"As you know, many years ago research showed that in animals certain polyunsaturated fatty acids were necessary and could not be synthesized from the diet or from the body by the body. And what happens is that when we lack this essential fatty acid, we get scaly skin and whole other changes in salts and the nervous system. These fats are also necessary for proper myelin-sheath formation, for nerve conduction. But you see, most of us have enough body fat that even if you don't eat any fat for many years, we can supply essential fatty acids from it. You understand?"

"Uh-huh."

"Now consequently, essential fatty acid deficiency was observed in animal studies and in children who were placed by their parents on an aberrant diet containing no fat. Now when long-term total parenteral alimentation is given, what actually happens is that the carbohydrate is high enough that insulin levels become quite high in the blood, and that prevents your body fat from being mobilized.

"And so, you got essential fatty acid deficiency not because you lacked the stores in your body fat, but because the carbohydrate is locking the fatty acid into the adipose tissue, your fat. And none is available in the circulating plasma because we're not infusing it. You see?"

"Yes, so you need to give me the fat again?"

"Yes. Dr. Kuksis of the Banting Institute, a lipid biochemist, has analyzed your blood for us and found that you have low levels of linoleic acid and excess of 22-polycarbon polyunsaturates. Together with the results of your liver biopsy we did on January 3, which showed fatty changes, and your liver function test results, which are more worrying to me, we've determined that you need fat. Up to now, we had heard that alimentation produces a fatty liver. No one quite knew what it was due to, and in the beginning, the kind of feeding we were doing on you, we didn't see any fatty liver. But now you have a fatty liver, and what our studies on you tell us is that the conventional thinking on this is wrong. Lipid *is* required to keep the fat out of the liver.

"So we're going to replace some of the carbohydrate with lipid, and we'll see what happens. We don't quite know what your fat requirement is, so we'll need to play around with it a bit. We'll start you off on 500 millilitres per day and see how that goes. If all goes well, we'll be able to discharge you in a few days. I've already spoken to Pharmacy about this. Okay?"

Judy nods. Finally, her skin will be healed! On the eleventh, Langer deals with her other chronic problem and changes her G-tube.

On January 12, Cliff drives down to TGH with trailer in tow to pick up Judy and her supplies. On her way out, Judy stops by Jeej's office and tells him that she wants to do something to thank him. He tells her that's not necessary, that her good health is thanks enough—and her cookies, too, of course. She laughs and tells him that's nonsense. She's going to throw a barbecue for him, his family, the GI ward staff, and the new alimentation patients. He graciously acquiesces and says he looks forward to it and to seeing where she lives. "I'll send you an invite and a map so you won't get lost," she tells him, waves good-bye, and continues down the hall with Cliff to the car and the brittle cold outside.

Chapter 17

Barbecue Season

Winter is long gone, and the summer sun and barbecue season have arrived. My parents tell us we're going to visit one of Daddy's patients in the country and hustle us into the blue Rambler. We soon leave the city and the wide 401 behind, as Daddy drives up the two-lane highway. I look out the window as he rounds a bend, the little posts with their reflective tops popping alongside us. He's explaining about this strange grown-up Judy, who's his patient, and how she's invited us all to a barbecue at her place. Pheroze is sitting beside me in the back of our car, and Mummy has Farida with her up in front along with Judy's detailed, hand-drawn map, complete with the location of the landmark beehive. I pepper him with questions: how much farther, does she have any children, is it on a lake? Mummy tells me to settle down; we'll soon be there. I look out my window again at the azure sky and scraggly evergreen Ontario wilderness.

Daddy slows the car as he turns onto a gravel road. Two horses are walking toward us, each carrying a girl with an unsmiling face and long, dark hair. I watch as they guide their horses to the side, noting the darkness within. Are they sad? Are they hostile? The girls look very old to me, and I wonder if they're Judy's children and why they're on the horses and not at the barbecue. But my thoughts are interrupted as Daddy pulls into a driveway in front of a small, one-storey clapboard house. We tumble out, and I immediately hide behind him. A tall woman with short, black hair and giant, brown-tinted granny glasses in slacks and a horizontally striped, short-sleeved top opens the door. A chubby tan-and-white dog bounds around from the side.

"Hi, Jeej!" she calls out and walks over to where we're standing beside the car. Her spreading smile transforms her characteristic North American face. "This must be Shireen," she says to me. I nod shyly, but her spirit washes over me, and soon I'm smiling back at her and stepping out from behind Daddy.

She leads us into her home and gives a short tour. She opens a closet and shows me an alien-looking vacuum cleaner with black puffy bags hanging down from the top and a thin steel tank sitting on the bottom. My curiosity propels me closer. She introduces this contraption as "Lester." She explains that this is where she eats. I stare and try to imagine how "Lester" feeds her.

"Would you like a cookie?" she asks me.

"Yes, please."

We all troop after Judy toward her tiny kitchen. She goes behind the white Formica counter, while we stay on the dining-room side, and takes out a tray of cookies from the oven and puts it on top of the stove. She slides a rack of cookies toward me across the counter.

"Go ahead, take a cookie. They're chocolate chip."

"Thank you." I pick up one of these rare treats and bite into it. Chocolate oozes between my teeth. I'm in heaven. Small, fits in the palm of my hand, chocolate and sugary sweetness, crunchy yet softly warm—I've never had anything so delicious. I know I'll have to ask Mummy to bake these. I finish my treat, and Judy tells me to help myself to another. But my mother tells me we have yet to eat lunch and not to fill myself up. I pout.

Quickly, Judy leads us out the back door to the lawn and the lake. She introduces us to the other adults, including Cliff, her husband. He is standing at the barbecue, its grill covered in burgers and hot dogs. "What do you want?" he asks me. I look up at Daddy, he nods, and I ask shyly if I can have a burger. Judy next introduces me to her daughter Miriam and shoos us off to play. Miriam asks if I want to see something. I nod, and she leads me out onto the dock. We look down through the clear lake water to the bottom. We see rocks and ripples of the sun and search for fish and turtles.

From far off, I hear, "Hey, Jeej, come help barbecue!"

"It's not everybody that gets their doctor cooking for them," Daddy chuckles in return. Laughter bursts the air.

I look over my shoulder to see my father flipping burgers, Miriam's father drinking a bottle of what looks like beer to me, and Judy and Mummy and other women sitting in woven, metal-framed patio chairs on the small square deck. The other women, Judy had said, are people like her, people who also have "Lesters" to feed them.

I return to looking for fish and turtles under the dock until we hear the call that our burgers and hot dogs are ready. We race to grab them. Judy tells us to help ourselves to her salads on the table nearby. More adults have arrived, and I recognize a couple I used to see at the hospital when Daddy would take me along to pick up some work and check up on patients. The doctors, nurses, and Judy and her fellow non-eaters talk shop.

When we're finished eating, Cliff asks, "You want to go water skiing?" I've never been water skiing before, and I want to go yet feel nervous. I look at Mummy, and she waves me to go.

"Come on. Miriam'll show you," Cliff urges me.

With a borrowed life jacket on, I watch Cliff pull Miriam around the lake, and then it's my turn. My feet hang off the dock, weighed down by these giant skis. I'll sink, I think. Cliff tells me to get down into the shallow water and let myself float with my feet at an angle to the water. I surprise myself by doing just that.

Miriam and Pheroze get in the boat with Cliff and sit facing me. Judy can't get in the boat because it isn't safe for her to get wet. She watches us all from her chair. I hang on tight to the handle, and slowly Cliff throttles up the motor. I feel myself rising, water falling off me in sheets. My arms pull taught, and my feet surface and flatten on top of the water. The boat's wake rises up on either side of me, and my skis create their own wash as my body slices through the air, flying toward the other side of the lake. Cliff turns to follow the curve of the land that juts out to the left of their cottage, and I'm heading for the boat's wake willy-nilly. I tense. Can I bounce over such large waves? I do! I bounce back into the middle, and too soon he's steering the powerful boat back to the dock. As we return to shore, I see Judy beaming at us, sharing our enjoyment of this adventure.

I'm wet and tired. The afternoon sun is waning, along with its warmth. I clamber out of the lake and race to the patio where my parents are sitting. "Can we ski at the cottage? Please!"

"We'll see," they reply. No amount of pleading will change their answer into an absolute promise, besides, they say, it's time to go. I don't want to leave. Judy's good spirit has me in her grip, and I find it difficult to detach myself. She hasn't stopped smiling ever, and her laughter has been the loudest and most contagious. She talks about doing this again next year since we all had so much fun. I grin at the idea, but still don't want to leave now. Next year is so far away. She seems to sense my disappointment and gives me another cookie for the road. Mollified, I climb into the car and settle onto the brocaded, blue cloth backseat. Dad slams the door shut, gets in, starts the car, and backs it out as Judy waves good-bye until we're out of sight. Pheroze and I fall asleep.

Chapter 18

The Bliss of Life

"I want to learn how to drive."

Cliff turns his eyes from the television set to Judy. "Pardon?" Her abrupt statement has caught him off guard. What is she going on about?

"I want to learn how to drive," Judy repeats over the clicking of her knitting needles. She looks steadily at him as she mindlessly rubs first one foot then the other. Her statement confounds him. This is going to surprise the hell out of Jeej, he thinks. It's surprising the hell out of him.

"The girls need to do more after school. 4-H will be good for them, and I can't enrol them unless I'm able to drive them when you're not here."

She isn't kidding, he realizes. "Okay," he says.

Judy learns quickly under Cliff's tutelage every evening, though she rarely hits the speed limit. She crawls along the highway, the two of them laughing at the honking and tooting cars piling up behind them, waving when they finally zip past her in the oncoming lane.

As soon as she has her driver's licence and her own car, she enrols Cyndy in 4-H to learn the necessities of life: cooking, sewing, and riding. Cyndy starts with cooking lessons at a neighbour's house. While the young teens giggle in the kitchen, Judy waits in the living room, rubbing her arms while chatting with the other mothers and sometimes with the host when she gets a moment until it's time to drive Cyndy home.

Judy likes the independence this new skill gives her, but she's not ready to extend it to driving to Toronto for the supply run, tests, and the occasional hospital visit. That's Cliff's job anyway. Still, she likes to maintain control over how those visits will go. One Tuesday afternoon, she writes on plain notepaper:

Jan. 16, 1973

Dear Dr. Jeejeebhoy;

I guess it is getting close to blood-testing time again? We are to pick up feeding on the tenth of February so—if you want to see me, could you make the appointment for sometime between the 5th and the tenth? Please ask Valerie to notify the pharmacy dept—Mrs. Cass Walsh—so they can have things ready.

Thank you,

Judy T.

P. S. Feeling fine—riding the snowmobile.

"That should get the wind up him," she chuckles to herself as she folds her letter in three and stuffs it into an envelope, reliving a similar kick she got out of sending him a photo of her on a motorbike. She'd just posed on it, but she hadn't told him that.

Her March supply run is also on a Saturday, also the tenth. She winds it up by visiting a patient new to alimentation, one who is not adjusting well. Her physician husband has left her—he cannot handle her illness—and she's preparing her alimentation, or "total parenteral nutrition" (TPN) as the medical team has now dubbed it, on her well-used bed as if avoiding infection doesn't matter anymore. Judy can't forget her all the way home. The next day, she writes hurriedly to Jeej after church:

Dear Dr. Jeejeebhoy,

Sorry I didn't bring this with me on Saturday. Too bad Beth can't snack like this little girl, it might help her to adjust a little better.

Judy Taylor

P. S. Tell Dr. Sanderson he didn't even leave a bruise.

Judy

She folds the letter in three and encloses the clipping from the *Atlanta Journal*, dated Sunday, January 28, 1973, about an eleven-year-old girl who is missing most of her intestines.

She had driven herself and her girls to church that morning. For the first couple of years up north, Cliff had driven them to Trinity United Church in Bobcaygeon and then waited for them outside until the end of the service. Now, he can stay at home in comfort. And she can volunteer at the church during the week. Serving others lifts her mood like nothing else and helps to distract her mind from her G-tube acid burns.

That G-tube agony propels her to write to Jeej on another Tuesday, her writing day:

March 27, 1973

Dear Dr. Jeejeebhoy,

Since you are so difficult to reach by telephone, I thought I'd write instead. My feeding is agreeing with me—just as you said it would—no problems. Could you let Kathy Ng [the clinical pharmacist] know so that pharmacy can make up enough until the twelfth of May?

We come in to see you again on the ninth of April, and I wondered if it would be possible to have my "G-tube" changed and the connection in my upper tube replaced (I think it is called an argyle.) The present one is rather loose. Valerie could let me know if this can be arranged.

Thanks a lot & we'll see you on the ninth.

Judy Taylor

Judy may not eat, but church life revolves around meals. Her hand is the first to shoot up to offer to cook a main course or to bake cookies. For Judy, every lunch or dinner function means another opportunity to cook, another opportunity to serve, another opportunity to watch others eat. It's one more opportunity to ask how it tastes and to sneak a chew herself and suck out all the flavour before spitting the remains out into a napkin. When the new minister, the Reverend Ed Bentley, arrives in 1976, he inspires her to lift her eyes up from the dinner table, her life's battleground, to see new ways of serving God. He quickly becomes her confidante and learns her story straight from her mouth, not through the usual grapevine as most of her neighbours do.

"I was so angry when this first happened to me," she dares to say as she finishes telling him how she got on TPN. "I asked God, 'Why me?'"

"This is a natural and healthy question. Grief generates a certain amount of energy. The energy is anger, but that doesn't have to be about something. It just is. The energy exists." He has noticed on Sundays how that energy becomes a direct connection to God for all those around her. She does not merely receive God's Grace, but she emits His goodness to anyone within range of her smile.

She is smiling at the reverend now as the weight of her guilt over her anger drops off in the light of his compassion. Encouraged, she relates how she came to start visiting others on G South in TGH and how she feels better as a result, especially when she advocates on their behalf to the doctors and nurses whom she knows so well.

"If you're angry about the circumstances of others, then you're less likely to be at risk of wallowing in your own pain," he affirms.

"Yes. Yes." She feels grateful that he understands and that she can share this hidden part of her. "I'm giving this as little power over my life as possible, and by God, my kids are going to have a normal life. I want to make sure they can grow up to be able to live on their own. I know I'm a control freak, and I've taken control of their timetable, but these girls would be lost without me being here. It's one reason why I had to learn how to drive." Judy decides that she's shared enough; it's starting to feel too real. She takes her leave, moving her mind onto choir practice that night.

Judy had joined the choir soon after she had learnt to drive. Singing fills her heart. The choir meets every Thursday night from seven to nine o'clock, and on those nights, she prepares her feeding up to the point of actually plugging it into her line so that when she returns home—her body tired yet racing with endorphins and happy, immune-fighting cells from singing with others—all she has to do is hook it up. At rehearsal, she inspires her fellow choristers. "Well, we better work on that," she jokes when they veer off key. And during the service, she smiles down steadily at the congregation from the stepped-up dais where the choir stands, raising a few smiles in return but not necessarily from all, which nettles her.

One of the gentleman choristers discreetly helps her back down the steps to the main floor after worship, whereupon she stops to scold a couple of familiar self-confident acquaintances. "You guys out there, singing, yet look at the faces on you. I'm so happy to be here. Why aren't you? I want to see you smiling back at me next Sunday."

She adds volunteering in the church office to her week. Her typing and telephone skills come in handy during the afternoons. She is a friendly voice at the church, for she loves to chat, to encourage others, and to help the occasional ill friend, even a boy she spoke to Jeej about seeing. And she can sit to do this work. She stands up only occasionally to wake her feet up when their tingling gets really annoying.

Judy joins Rev. Bentley's pastoral-care team, for not only is she a natural at visiting those in hospital, but she gets another night out, another way to get out of her own head. He teaches the team members how to be good listeners and how to visit those who are hurting. Once a week, Judy accompanies one of the other team members to the hospital in Lindsay. They sit down beside the hospitalized parishioner, and Judy leans forward to talk. Her smile, her hazel eyes, her attitude of unconditional listening and giving put the patient at ease. She talks about the patient's experiences, not her own, and she calms the patient down, but when it's time to pray, she takes a backseat to her partner.

Judy normally doesn't think too much about her appearance, but her hair had turned fine and fly away after 1970, and it has frustrated her ever since. She's not skilled at styling, and she'd rather use her energy for other things. She tells a friend how difficult it is to control her hair.

"Oh, you should try Joyce," the woman tells her.

"She'll know how to deal with this hair?"

"Definitely," she responds, and she gives Judy directions.

Judy wants to look nice on Sunday mornings. Because Cliff likes her around when he's at home, and she hates sitting alone at home when the children are at school and he's at work, she makes an appointment for Fridays.

Joyce's salon is in her two-storey home. A large sign above the garage announces: "Joyce's Hairstyling." Judy enters. Joyce is blow-drying one woman's hair, another is sitting under a dryer, and a third is flipping through a magazine. Judy doesn't know any of them.

Joyce calls out, "Hello!"

"Hello!" Judy calls back and starts talking to all. She doesn't once think about the odd problems multiplying in her body, problems Jeej doesn't understand and has to research. When it's her turn to sit in the chair, she tells Joyce how hard her hair is to style but that she'd like it to look nice.

Joyce looks it over. The hair is like a two-year-old's hair, fine and prone to sticking out. She can tell that Judy doesn't have much desire or skill to style it. She suggests setting it in rollers. Over the years, she will try other methods of controlling Judy's hair. Tight perms last only six to eight weeks because Judy's new growth is fly-away hair. The wind undoes sets in one blow. And blow-dryers and curling irons prove as ineffective. One thing Judy never has to worry about, though, is grey hair.

Joyce talks as she snips. She concentrates when she gets to the nape of the neck. The skin wrinkles under the pressure of the scissors as she cuts across. It feels like rubber. She says nothing to Judy, wanting to let her keep her dignity.

"There!" she announces. She holds up a mirror and turns Judy so Judy can see her hair from all angles.

Judy's smile widens. Despite her fatigue from the outing, Judy leaves feeling uplifted by her new do.

Once home, she opens her front door with relief. She has time to rest before cooking and serving dinner. Afterward, she retires to the living room with Cliff. They sit in their chairs in front of the television, her knitting needles going and her Intralipid dripping into her vein under gravity. It empties after three hours, and she hooks up the Amigen portion of her TPN. It's late now, and on Intralipid nights, she doesn't stay up to watch the Amigen drip in for the usual two hours. She rolls up her knitting, puts it in its bag, and pushes Lester on his Sheppard casters, which Cliff had installed, across the indoor-outdoor carpeting to the bedroom. She changes into her nightclothes and moves into the bathroom. Cliff stays rooted in his chair, staring at the TV screen, for he wants no part of the ugly mess that's about to be revealed.

She carefully peels off the dressing from over her G-tube. She soaks a cotton wipe in Detergicide and strokes it over her screaming skin until all the spillage from her stomach is gone. The pain, as of a thousand cigarette burns, never lets up. She swipes up gobs of Garamycin cream and dabs it on as tears flow down her cheeks. She unstraps the leg bag, pushes it in, and takes it off her G-tube. She drapes it over the side of the tub, next to the bed-bag tubing that's been draining all day. She picks it up and pushes it on. She puts a disposable bag on the end of the tubing and throws it over Lester. She exhales deeply.

She grabs a tissue, wipes her eyes so that Cliff won't see, and pushes Lester to the bedroom. Cliff joins her. She throws the disposable bed bag on to the floor and climbs into bed. She reaches for her Bible and turns to her passage for the night. Grateful for the extra day of life she has just been given, she studies the passage, focusing on what God is trying to tell her, on what she needs to learn. Cliff vigilantly watches the solution dripping steadily into her Langer Line.

Finished with her reading, she turns off the light, but Cliff uses some reflected light from the plastic to keep an eye on her in case she flings an arm out and pulls her line. Judy sleeps.

Two hours later, Cliff is sleeping, and Judy's bladder wakes her up, filled from the constant *drip drip drip* of the Amigen. She obeys its urgent call, picking up her bed bag and throwing it over Lester before heading down the hall. While in the bathroom, she takes the opportunity to start the stopwatch for one minute and to count the drips. There should be fifty to sixty drops per minute. It's running too fast. She adjusts it and counts the drips for another minute to ensure it's running at the proper rate, after which she stamps her feet to try and get feeling back in them and returns to bed for another two hours of sleep before her bladder wakes her up yet again.

Cyndy hears the clank of the air tank and the squeak of the wheels returning to Judy's bedroom, turns over, and falls back asleep.

Chapter 19

JJ, the Guinea Pig

It had all started back in 1972. Five months after Jeej had put her back on Intralipid and four months after he'd added choline to her infusion, he'd called Judy back into TGH on June 4, 1972, to evaluate the effects of the choline. She had left the hospital on June 17 with a new Amigen source, unbeknownst to her. The old source was casein; the new source was synthetic, which would give her more methyl-donating groups. Unfortunately, the doctors didn't realize that casein, unlike the synthetic source, contaminates the Amigen with electrolytes and trace elements, the kind Judy needs, the kind researchers and physicians didn't know much about in 1972. The new Amigen beefed her up and made her skin elastic and dry.

It's October 1973, and Judy starts losing weight. Each week, she sheds a pound. By Monday, December 3, she has lost five kilograms. Jeej is not happy. He admits her to I South to investigate. (The GI and TPN programs have expanded so much that they now occupy two wards: I West and I South in the College Wing of TGH.)

She is not happy with the familiar battery of blood, urine, and G-tube collection tests, and the unfamiliar, exotic tests two days later tense her up even more.

She is taken to the basement for the first test and waits outside a room that looks like a cold war fallout shelter while the radiologist measures the radiation the room is emitting. When he is done, he sends her into the steel-lined space and clangs the door shut. The steel was salvaged from pre-WWII battleships, built before the first atomic bombs exploded, before we puffed radiation into the earth's air and soaked new steel with it. It has little radiation of its own, and it keeps radiation out, the kind that comes from cosmic rays that bombard us all the time and excite the potassium in our cells to morph into potassium-40. Knowing how much potassium-40 Judy has will tell Jeej how much lean body mass she has.

71

There is no upper limit to the amount of mass, but there is a lower limit. A number below this limit indicates that she is wasting.

The radiologist counts the radioactive waves emitting from Judy as she sits. Nothing to it, right? But then, Jeej wants to flood her with radiation.

In another room, she clambers onto a sliding bed. Underneath it sits a container of beryllium. Overhead is a detector coated in wax. The bed slides her over the beryllium as it pumps slow neutrons into her body, which shoot through her and stop dead at the wax barrier. Her cells, stimulated by the neutrons, emit gamma rays. Those rays penetrate the wax, and the detector counts the gamma rays. The results tell Jeej how much nitrogen her body contains and thus how much protein.

Jeej reviews her tests and decides to reduce her IV thyroxine. Langer changes her G-tube, and Judy gains two kilograms. It seems like they've solved the problem.

Cliff picks her up on December 8, a Saturday, to take her home. He no longer waits for her in town during her hospital stays. He goes back home to work after he's dropped her off and avoids the hospital as much as possible.

"Jeej, I'm walking on cotton wool," Judy announces on the next supply run.

"You're what?" Jeej raises his eyebrows.

"Walking on cotton wool. And my toes feel frozen and fat. What are you going to do about it?"

"How long has this been going on?" he asks. And as he listens, he puts his hand up to his mouth, while his other hand supports his elbow. His eyes watch her intently. He notices that she is unsteady. This is a huge problem, he thinks. He checks her nitrogen balance study carefully. She's in the negative. Not good. He increases her calories from 1,900 to 2,500.

The months slip by with no news from Jeej. One February night in 1974, Judy looks at her line for a long moment. "Cliff, it's not dripping."

His heart leaps. She's going to die. His fear has become real. Only he can get her down to Jeej fast enough to save her. Damn the Air Force. That plane from CFB Trenton will take too long to get to them. He jumps out of his chair to get the car, while Judy unhooks herself from the TPN. He dashes back into the house and hustles her to the car. He speeds down the deserted highways to TGH. He squeals into the ER. They rush in and ask for Jeej. He's not there, but Johnston is on duty and with brute force dislodges a clot from the end of her catheter. This line is only a month old. He and Langer had put it in when her old line had developed a kink, got jammed in scar tissue, snapped off when they tried to remove it, and left a piece stuck to her jugular. They had threaded a new Silastic catheter in through her cephalic vein and felt that the rogue piece would not cause any infections, just as a pacemaker lead that breaks off does no harm.

Her new line clear again, he tells her to increase her heparin for a week and then to reduce it back down to her regular levels while increasing the amount of water she uses to irrigate it. Cliff worries even more about her during the next feeding. But Judy smiles, relieved at being given one more day.

Finally, Jeej brings Judy back into hospital on April 2 to find out why her weight shows no increase and why her G-tube discharge smells awful. He asks a neurologist to do an EMG on her. The neurologist diagnoses peripheral neuropathy from diabetes. Jeej cannot believe it and orders an IV glucose tolerance test during the day and another at night while she is infusing. Sure enough, she is most definitely diabetic. Yet she has no family history of diabetes and no earlier indication of this condition. Why has she become diabetic?

He spots another problem. She is receiving too much vitamin D. He had based her daily intake on what humans normally need—four hundred units per day minimum. But it seems that the five hundred units in her TPN was a tad high. While instructing the pharmacy to add insulin for Judy's diabetes, he also asks them to have her alternate her MVI with Soluzyme, which contains no vitamin D, in order to cut her average daily intake down to two hundred and fifty units.

With relief, Judy believes that Jeej finally knows what her problem is. She'll be fine. And she's thankful to finally be going home on April 17. But she had not liked being gastroscoped. She says to Cliff on the drive home, "I told Jeej I'm never doing that again."

Judy's fame is reaching beyond the hospital walls, and she's quite surprised to receive a phone call from Bill Trent of *Weekend Magazine*, which appears Saturdays in Canada's national newspaper, *The Globe and Mail*. He wants to spend a few hours with her. On the big day, she scoots the children off, only allowing them back into the house when Bill asks to speak with them. The girls know to keep up the fiction of normalcy, and Judy plans to show him that she can do anything. She even climbs onto her girls' pony, but she does so stiffly, unable to feel the stirrups with her fuzzy feet. She laughs it off by saying that this is what diabetes does to you and slides off, her family holding their breath in fear of her falling.

Trent's lengthy article soon appears, and ABR acquires over a hundred copies of the June 22, 1974, edition to dole out to us, the nurses, doctors, fellow lab researchers, lab techs, and anyone else he can think of. Toronto and Bobcaygeon buzz with this new public fame for what Jeej and Judy are doing.

Jeej basks only briefly in the limelight. His August vacation over, he has work to do. The insulin did not solve her neuropathy, and this worries him. This is not normal diabetes. Something else is going on.

He looks for an answer in the piles of research journals that perch precariously wherever he has room for them both at his office and at his home. And there, in one of the journals, he finds a possible explanation in an article written by W. Mertz, an animal biologist. His heart quickens. He has his secretary track down the man's phone number.

"I read your paper on how you found chromium promotes insulin action," he says to Mertz. He goes on to explain Judy's symptoms and her lack of response to her insulin infusion. Mertz's description of the marks of chromium deficiency seems to fit Judy. "Do you know of any human cases?"

"No, none. I'm not sure what to say about your interesting problem. I've never heard of it, but I'm not a physician."

Jeej thanks him and hangs up. The more he thinks about it, the more compelling he finds Mertz's research. He has his secretary call Judy to schedule another experiment.

"He's using me as a guinea pig again," Judy tells Cliff that night.

"Jeej seems to be doing a lot of tests on you."

"Well, it is for the sake of science. They're learning. I'll let them do it." The click of her knitting needles pauses. "I'm a guinea pig," she guffaws. "Maybe I'll get him a guinea pig for Christmas instead of the zipper I was thinking of for all those surgeries he's done on me!"

Later that month, as Cliff drives out of the College Wing parking lot toward the service entrance, Judy walks into the hospital carrying her Christmas present for Jeej, as well as her usual cookie tins, and makes her way to his office. She sits down in his waiting room, the cloth-draped cage on her lap, and talks non-stop with Valerie, Jeej's secretary, until Jeej emerges from his office. Judy stands up and offers him her gift. "I'm tired of being a guinea pig Jeej. Here, there's one for you to use."

Jeej takes it, astonished. He lifts a corner of the cloth and sees a tan-and-white guinea pig, eyes closed, lying on newspapers. "Well, thank you," he says nonplussed.

"His name is JJ," she says, waiting to see how long it will take him to pick up on the name. Not long. He chuckles. He likes that acronym for Judy and Jeej. He puts the cage down as she hands him his tin of cookies. Before munching on one, he tells her why he wants to admit her in January. He has a plan for her fuzzy feet. She understands and leaves to visit the ward. Hours later, he picks up the cage and carries it home.

"Olive!" he shouts as he opens the front door of his still-new-smelling, recently renovated house. Pheroze and I are already waiting for him, for I had seen him coming up the walk through the front windows with this mysterious thing in his hand.

"What is it, Khush? I'm in the middle of dinner!" she shouts back from the kitchen.

"You've got to come and see this." She doesn't respond, so we shout for her to come, eager to see what he has brought. Finally, she rushes into the hall, wiping her hands.

"You won't believe what I got today." He removes the cloth from over the cage, revealing the guinea pig snuffling round inside.

"What's his name?" I ask.

"Can I have it?" Pheroze asks.

"Sure." He hands Pheroze the cage while Mum admonishes my brother about having to look after it. Mouthing the eager promises of a seven-year-old, he disappears upstairs.

Unfortunately, JJ has a short life. In the spring, my mother picks dandelion leaves for JJ from our front yard, not knowing our neighbour had vigorously sprayed all of hers with pesticide, which had wafted over to our lawn. After feasting on his treat, JJ looks a bit green and then goes comatose. He dies.

Chapter 20

Chromium Deficiency and the Swedish Professor

In the April 1977 issue of the *American Journal of Clinical Nutrition*, Jeej's article on chromium deficiency appears. As lead author, he had written this paper with ABR, Dr. Richard Chu, Dr. Errol Marliss, and Dr. Gordon Greenberg. Although he does not realize just how groundbreaking his discovery is and how heavily cited this paper will become by other researchers and the American Diabetes Association even thirty years later, he is thrilled about his finding and excitedly shares his story with Wretlind, a man he regards highly, a man who himself did pioneering research in parenteral nutrition and is responsible for the development of Intralipid, a man whose work Jeej had read when devising Judy's original alimentation. Wretlind has come to Canada to visit Jeej and Judy and sits now with Jeej in his College Wing office.

"We gave her the insulin. It increased her weight, but she didn't at all improve. And frankly, I didn't know what was wrong with her for a whole year." Jeej flings his hands wide and raises his eyebrows to emphasize his point.

His audience listens, enraptured. Wretlind has flown all the way from Sweden to see for himself what this remarkable physician and his unique patient are doing, to see just how they're revolutionizing TPN, the name Jeej used to describe this artificial feeding in his seminal article on Judy in the 1973, Vol. 65 issue of *Gastroenterology*, which Jeej had read in part in front of the Ninth International Congress of Nutrition in Mexico City in September 1972.

Jeej continues, "When I was reviewing this whole trace element stuff, I came across the fact that chromium was required to promote insulin action. Well, I called Mertz, the animal biologist with the USDA, the United States Department of Agriculture. I spoke to him, and I asked him, 'Do you know of any human cases?' And he said none. So I thought about this for a while. And, you know, I found his work so compelling, I just went ahead and gave her, Judy, the chromium, and it worked." Jeej leans forward, his face still showing disbelief at this miracle cure.

"It worked?"

"The results were absolutely dramatic." He leans back and flings his hands out. "Absolutely dramatic. Her glucose intolerance went away, and her neuropathy disappeared."

"This is an important achievement, Khush!"

"We were all very excited. As you know, for a long time, people didn't know why she was having all this trouble. Then we knew that chromium worked in animals. But it is one of those types of trace elements where the data is elusive in showing what chromium does. We can show it in adipose tissue slices. We can show it in animal-type studies. But it's very difficult to show that chromium has any value in diabetes."

"I agree. Is not the absorption of the inorganic form very low?"

"Yes, you're right. The organic form, called 'glucose tolerance factor,' well … we don't know its composition. You get it from yeast. There's lots of chromium in yeast, but we couldn't give Judy yeast!"

Wretlind laughs, "No."

"Now, if you take a diabetic, you got to feed him. But his food is not going in an IV. So we could give Judy the inorganic form."

"You didn't have to worry about absorption," Wretlind states the obvious.

"No," Jeej smiles. Coming from a long line of storytellers, he loves telling stories, but this one is particularly sweet. "It went right into her bloodstream. Within three days, her stores of chromium built to the saturation point, and her plasma glucose fell almost to normal. We were floored."

"How did you measure her chromium levels?"

"Well, we measured them, but you know the blood tests are really useless. See, chromium measurements have been very tricky because they're done by atomic absorption spectroscopy. You change all these trace elements into a volatile vapour, but as you know, chromium volatilizes at 2,400 degrees centigrade. See? And the problem is that when chromium is in tissues, the heating of the tissues themselves produces a kind of smoke. And that confuses the reading of the chromium. We couldn't do the measurements ourselves."

Wretlind raises his eyebrows.

"No, we had to send her blood away to Richard Chu out in Albany, New York. He did all the measurements for us. ABR—you've met my colleague in the lab at the university?"

Wretlind indicates he has.

"Well, he got together all her samples of urine, G-tube drainage collections, blood, and even the tap water she drinks and sent them off to Dr. Chu at the Veteran Administration Hospital in Albany in October 1974. What we didn't know at the time was that her blood levels didn't reflect the tissue levels. And taking her blood was a big problem. There's chromium in needles, so we had to use only plastic. We also had her hair analyzed. Then when we brought her in for the infusion, we had no idea what would happen, how much chromium we should even give. So we brought her into the hospital for a week so we could watch her for the metabolic effects. We knew once we started infusing chromium directly into her bloodstream, her blood levels would mean nothing."

"Yes."

"We were looking for changes in her neuropathy, for a biological effect. And that's what we found. A rapid biological effect! For the whole year, she had been monitored, and no change had occurred with the insulin. Then we give her chromium, and there was a dramatic change in her response to insulin. It definitely got better. We took an initial sample to test her plasma clearance of intravenously administered glucose when we first admitted her; then we infused 250 micrograms of chromium per day from January 7 to January 21."

"This was in 1975?"

"Yes, and her blood sugar just fell. We didn't have to give her insulin anymore. We'd actually stopped it earlier so we could test the chromium without added insulin interfering with the results."

"Amazing."

"What was interesting was that our findings suggested that, up to this point, fat was being used as a major source of energy despite all the glucose and insulin we were giving her, so she had a markedly raised level of free fatty acids. But after only seven days on chromium, her free fatty acid levels dropped, and she was now using both carbohydrate and fat for energy. Furthermore, after only three days, she began to excrete increasing amounts of chromium. She had reached her maximum retention of chromium in only three days, and that's the same period when her plasma glucose fell to within normal range."

"How did you decide how much to give her?"

"Well, what we did was ... I looked at what were the levels of chromium in the tissue. I looked at some idea of what the depletion could have been. And we realized later, you know, that when we switched her to synthetic amino acids, we essentially lost a lot of the trace elements that had been piggybacking in the original casein-sourced alimentation."

"I see."

"So now we knew that with the synthetic source of amino acids, Judy was no longer getting trace elements that she had been before, and the most dramatic example of that was the chromium. So we gave her what I thought was an approximation for that purpose. After that we put her on a smaller dose, about 20 micrograms per day, in her home TPN."

"When I heard about your studies in man, I stopped all further investigations in dogs because you've proved conclusively that my opinion was right. This chromium study is just further proof that you are the father of TPN."

Jeej demurs.

Wretlind insists and continues, "And now I will be going to meet this wonderful lady. I will be able to tell my colleagues that I personally have seen this patient." Marlene Close, the nurse manager now working with Jeej, had told Wretlind about Judy at the September 1979 First Congress of the ESPEN (the European Society for Clinical Nutrition and Metabolism), and he's been eager to meet her ever since. He hands back the photo of Judy on her pony that Jeej had shown him when he had first sat down in his office.

"You will like her. Now, you have a map and know how to get there?"

"Yes, thank you, Khush. I've enjoyed our talk immensely."

Wretlind finds his rental car, reviews his map, and drives out of TGH's parking lot toward Highway 401 East and Judy's house.

As soon as he parks in her driveway, Judy opens the front door and steps out smiling. She cannot believe that this professor has flown all the way over from Sweden and driven two hours in an unfamiliar country just to see her.

He notices immediately that she is in perfect shape.

She welcomes him in, shows off Lester, sits him down in her tidy living room, and serves him tea.

"Thank you, Mrs. Taylor, for having me. I've been looking forward to meeting you. I've heard and read about your successful TPN and HPN for several years now. This is certainly an important achievement from a medical point of view. Thanks to you and Dr. Jeejeebhoy, you have proven my old hypothesis right, that TPN or HPN properly administered is an adequate alternative to oral food in a patient without an intestinal tract. Now, please tell me about your experiences."

She tells him, feeling awed and proud that this university professor, this inventor of her Intralipid, is sitting in her living room, drinking her tea, interested in her experience and her thoughts on Intralipid.

He sees how mentally and emotionally, not just physically, healthy she is. She seems not to be affected by her home TPN at all. She is not suffering, he marvels. Too soon, the hours are up, and he must be off.

"I would like you to come one day to visit us in Sweden." He wants to show her off, to prove to his colleagues that patients on home TPN can be in good health and that home TPN can be a good alternative to food.

Judy cannot see how that is possible. She has never been out of the country, and she has Lester. Still, she is thrilled. "I would love to!"

"That is good."

They shake hands, and Judy walks him to his car. She waves until he's no longer in sight. She goes back inside, closes the door, and lies down on the couch before it's time to cook dinner.

Chapter 21

At the Police Station

"Cyndy, my GP needs a full-time babysitter for her two children this summer, someone to cook and shop for her during the day while she works," Judy announces to her eldest. "I'll help you cook, and you can call me if you have any trouble. I'll drive you down every morning."

Cyndy shrugs. It is a chance to have a real job and earn real money. Besides, what her mother says goes.

The summer starts off well. Judy helps Cyndy cook spaghetti sauce and bake cookies in the evenings and then package them up for transport the next day. She drives her daughter down to the doctor's home in the mornings, and while Cyndy puts away the food, Judy chats briefly with her GP. Cathy had introduced Judy to her when she'd first moved up north. She takes care of Judy's tests when Jeej wants some done, and Jeej keeps her informed as to how Judy is doing with any nutritional difficulties. Finally, Judy has an opportunity to give back. Having Cyndy babysit her GP's children supports the doctor in her new role as a single parent and benefits Cyndy by giving her a chance to earn her own spending money. Judy sees it as a win-win situation for everybody.

One day, the doctor nips back home to check on her children and Cyndy and finds it empty. She stands in her living room, thinking about where a teenaged girl would want to be on a sunny summer day. The fairgrounds! She finds them behind the arena. Cyndy has met up with two young men, and the three are smoking pot, a rather 1970s thing to do. She blasts Cyndy, her worry and racing adrenaline adding fuel to her outrage. She has zero tolerance for drug use, any drug use, especially in front of her kids. She takes their hands and leads them off, assuring Cyndy that she will be phoning her mother.

Judy's heart sinks when she hears her GP's angry voice on the other end of the telephone. Judy assures her that she has the situation under control. After hanging up, she waits for Cyndy. As she waits, her mind wanders. She starts thinking about these last few years on TPN and how it's affected her family. She starts recalling memories of Cyndy before all this trouble began, and they bring a smile to her face.

Judy recalls the first time she'd tried to discipline Cyndy after coming home from the hospital. She'd been sitting on the couch, unable to get up, angry at her daughter. She had told Cyndy to come and stand in front of her so that she could spank her. Cyndy complied. As she'd raised her hand, Cyndy stepped forward.

"Come back here. I'm going to hit you," Judy commanded.

Cyndy stepped back, and as Judy once again raised her hand, she snickered and said, "No, you're not," and stepped forward.

"Get back here!" Judy saw blood.

But again, Cyndy stepped out of reach, sniggering.

The futility of trying to spank her teenaged daughter when she couldn't rise from the couch or chase her started Judy's belly shaking. She tried to control it, but her laugh bubbled out, and the two howled.

Judy smiles at that memory before her eyes refocus on her surroundings. She wonders what has happened between then and today. She puts her hand on her side to hold her G-tube still, puts her other hand on the chair arm to leverage herself up, and stands up slowly. She walks to the window to look out for Cyndy. She prays.

It does not go well that night. Cyndy soon runs away to the circus, the dream of many a kid in the 1970s, and becomes a ticket seller. She moves from town to town until she ends up in a camping site near Bobcaygeon. She's hungry and has no money. She goes to the local IGA and charges groceries on the GP's charge account, counting on the cashier not knowing that she no longer works for the doctor.

But when the doctor sees the charges on her bill, she calls the police, who find Cyndy and charge her with theft.

"She's where?" Judy hangs up in disbelief. "Cliff, Cyndy's in jail in Lindsay. We have to go bail her out." Cliff grabs the car keys and storms out of the house with Judy in his wake as, wide-eyed, Julie and Miriam watch them leave.

At the police station, they ask the officer on duty about Cyndy. He fetches the arresting officer, who explains what had happened and what Cyndy's been charged with.

"What should we do?" Judy asks him.

"Well, ma'am, it's your decision."

"What do you recommend we do? Should we bail her out?"

"Well, I'd leave her there. That's the best thing you can do. She won't learn anything if you bail her out. Leave her for a good two or three days; that might sink it in to her. Then come back." He doesn't know the history of this family. To him, she's just another rebellious teenager.

They discuss his suggestion briefly and agree. They ask to see her. He leads them to the cells, where Cyndy leaps thankfully to the bars when she sees them.

She cannot believe it when they tell her that they won't be bailing her out. The visit ends quickly, with Cyndy calling out to Judy's retreating back, "Don't leave me here. Don't leave me again!" The outer door bangs shut, and she's alone without her mother.

The drive home in the dark is endless. Judy decides to call her GP the next day to apologize. She feels embarrassed that her desire to help has ended so badly. Then she wonders if they've done the right thing leaving Cyndy in jail. Her worry erupts as they drive along the pitch-black rural highway, their headlights the only thing lighting up what's ahead of them.

"I feel bad, Cliff."

"I know, but the cop said it was the better way to go."

She starts crying.

"I know it isn't the right thing to do as a parent, but on the other hand ..." He lets the thought go unfinished.

Bailed out several days later by her employer, Cyndy returns home, but runs away again when Judy has to go into the hospital for some tests. When he returns home from work and discovers her gone, Cliff tells Julie to get in the car—they're going to go look for Cyndy and bring her back before Judy finds out. But Cyndy runs away again after Judy returns home. Cliff and Julie find her once again and bring her back. She keeps running. Cliff steams more with each episode, with each time he or the police hunt her down, with each time he sees Judy's broken heart dissolving in sobs when Cyndy takes off. He's not happy with that, for he had told the girls when he brought Judy home back in 1971 not to upset their mother. Now, practically every night, Judy is crying and getting on the phone to the prayer chain to ask them to pray for Cyndy. Finally, he tells Judy that he doesn't want to bring her back.

"We'll give her another try," she says.

"Well, I don't think we should, because she's just going to upset you again."

"She's doing this because of something I've done. If this hadn't happened to me, Cyndy would be all right. I've got to try to get her on the right track."

Julie reassures her mom that nothing she has done is the reason for Cyndy's troubles. What she cannot voice is that for Cyndy, as for Julie and Miriam, loving their mom is fraught with danger. The penalty for loving their mom is the knowledge that each day might be the last day they'll see her, that she will abandon them again just like she did back in 1970, and that this abandonment might be permanent. Perhaps it's safer to be the ones to leave and to find love elsewhere—except they do not know how to do so without risk to themselves.

Cliff reaches his limit. Judy is taking days to recover from Cyndy's running. The emotions unbalance her routine, and he doesn't want her to die. He didn't fight for her all those long, miserable months to lose her now because of their eldest daughter. As he waits once more with Judy for the police to find Cyndy, he makes a decision and tells Judy that Cyndy must leave. They argue. He agrees to talk to his old employer about giving Cyndy a job, and so Judy agrees to call her sister in Toronto and have Cyndy stay with her.

Judy jumps when she hears the thunderous knock on the door. She grabs her side and walks to the door as quickly she can. She opens it and light spills out onto the tableau awaiting her. Cyndy stands between two officers, her long, black hair straggling down her tall body. Judy reaches for her daughter, bringing her in from the night, tears streaming down her face.

Ever mindful of where it's safe to put her arms, Cyndy hugs her mom gingerly and sobs on her shoulder. Judy leads her in to the living room and orders Julie and Miriam to bed. When alone, Judy and Cliff tell Cyndy their plans.

"You can't come home anymore," Cliff informs Cyndy.

"You don't love me!" Cyndy shouts back in the familiar teenage refrain. "Nobody loves me! Why do you always pick on me, Dad?" She inhales raggedly.

"'Cause you're upsetting your mother!"

"Cyndy, he's not picking on you. He just wants you to stay in school and stop running away."

"You love everybody else more than me!"

"You can't upset your mother no more!" Cliff shouts at Cyndy.

The row lasts late into the night. The next day, Cliff packs up her suitcase in the car, frogmarches her into the passenger seat, drives her to the bus station, buys her a one-way ticket to Toronto, watches her get on the bus, watches the bus leave, and drives home. He will never forgive her for devastating Judy. It isn't the thievery or the running away or the drug use that infuriates and terrifies him; it is the toll on Judy.

"She's on the bus," Cliff tells Judy as he walks back into the house. "I don't want you calling her now. It'll only upset you." He sits in his chair and disappears behind the newspaper. Judy finds solace in her kitchen as she makes plans to contact Cyndy without Cliff knowing and getting all upset.

Chapter 22

More Family Trouble

It's Miriam's turn to row with Cliff. It's a nightly thing, and she's starting to feel guilty about it, not because of the conflict itself, but because of how it's affecting her mother. Judy steps out of the kitchen to try to make peace, as she usually does. One of her rules is to not talk about it, whatever the problem is, unless you have to. These two are violating her rule loudly and dragging her down. She has been feeling well since Jeej had cleared up all her nutritional deficiencies and feeling more settled since Cyndy had left a few years earlier. But now, these two stubborn and so-alike members of her family are bringing chaos back into her life. She says to Miriam about this latest contretemps, "We'll work it out. Don't worry. I'll talk to your father." To Cliff she says, "We'll talk about this later." The two separate.

In the cool light of the following morning, Miriam decides to put an end to the fighting. She speaks to her friend in Fenelon Falls and not long after she moves in with her friend's family in order to give her mom a break and to make biking to work easier.

With Miriam gone, the house quietens down. Judy and Cliff revert to their routines. It's 1978, and Cliff has left his oil-burner job to become a manager in a lumber store. Tuesday is his day off. He looks outside at the fine weather and sees it's a good time to clean the bow window that faces the lake. It's fiddly work, cleaning a multitude of little mullions, and it takes him all day. Near supper time, he empties the dirty water, puts his tools away, cleans up, and collapses in his chair, thankful to be done. He picks up the paper to read what his favourite football team, the Toronto Argonauts, is up to, but after a few lines, he realizes he doesn't remember a thing. He starts over. He starts again. Now, he can't pronounce the words. In frustration, he screws up the paper and throws it on the floor. Judy peers out from the kitchen, but says nothing. She calls him to the table, and they eat in silence. He cannot say words out loud. When she brings dessert to the table, she shows him the whipped cream can and asks him, "What's that?"

He shakes his head. That hurts.

"It's whipped cream." She pauses briefly and asks, "What is it?"

He doesn't know. He pushes back his chair, deciding to go straight to bed. He has a tremendous headache. It's gripped him for forty-five minutes. Suddenly, it leaves. He sleeps. Unbeknownst to him, the clot has just left his brain.

Judy stays mum the next morning, knowing if she says anything he will refuse to heed her advice just to be contrary. Even though he has regained his speech, Cliff feels exhausted and makes an appointment to see Dr. John Da Costa, their new GP (the previous one had moved out of the area). Da Costa tells him not to work until he has a dye study and an EEG done. It'll take about two or three months to book him for the dye study, but he refers him to Peterborough for an EEG that week. Cliff tells Judy that night that he has to wait for the big test and cannot work until then. She is having none of that. She phones Jeej.

Within a week, Cliff is being wheeled into the OR at TGH under the care of a top neurologist. After reviewing his test results, the neurologist tells him to take two aspirin a day and a water pill and not to let anyone change these orders. Da Costa had already told him to start jogging, which he does faithfully every night after supper, six to eight kilometres. Meanwhile, he stays off work for a month and accompanies Judy on her usual errands. In Zellers department store, Judy stops to chat to a strange woman. Cliff stays rooted near the cart. Judy and the woman part, and Judy returns to Cliff's side.

"Why didn't you come over and speak to Shirley?" she asks Cliff.

"Who is Shirley?"

"Jim's wife. You worked for him for two or three years."

"Oh." Cliff remembers now.

They look at each other silently. He's lost his memory for faces but not for names. Judy has already changed her cooking style—skinning the chicken breasts, feeding him rice every night, preparing low-fat meals, and ensuring he eats dinner at the same time. Today, she decides that when in public she'll whisper "You remember so and so" so that he will know who they're bumping into and can say hello like normal. She also pesters him to move into town to be safer. They do, but Judy feels claustrophobic in Bobcaygeon proper, and time heals her fear of losing him. Two years later, they move back to the lake into a bigger house. Life settles down again.

Julie, their now-twenty-one-year-old middle daughter, pops in for a visit. Judy and she sit and chat, just the two of them. Judy unburdens onto Julie her latest worry, knowing that Julie will blow off whatever she tells her and will not hold a grudge when Judy lets go of her anger and moves on. Julie keeps her face neutral as she listens. They hear the door open, and in walks Cliff. A grin crawls across his face when he sees Julie. He joins them, and the conversation turns to lighter topics. Judy fills the space with her bold laughter, while Julie smiles her shy smile, and Cliff natters away. It's pleasant even when a natural silence between topics grows.

"I'm pregnant," Julie announces.

Judy and Cliff stare at their unwed daughter, who has always been a rock for Judy.

Julie looks at the rug. She has been putting off this moment for as long as possible, but at five months along, she fears an observant neighbour will tell her mother.

Cliff retires into silence. But Judy speaks her mind. "Julie, how can you be so stupid!"

Julie says nothing.

"You don't know how disappointed I am in you. Who's the father?"

"Gord, of course," Julie replies, pronouncing the name of her live-in boyfriend.

"You should marry him before the baby is born."

"No, I don't think that's a good idea, Mom. So many people get married in these situations, and then their marriages don't last. Then all you hear about is how they only married because of the baby. I definitely don't want that, and I don't want Gord in that situation either."

Judy says nothing.

"If I can't afford to take care of it, we could put it up for adoption." Julie offers this olive branch to her mother, for it goes without saying that abortion is a non-starter. Not only is her mom dead set against it, but she has also many a time told her family about how lucky she feels for having been adopted and not aborted, for having been given a chance at life.

"Well, if that's the way to go, I'll help you as far as finding out who you can talk to."

When she enters the church office later that week, Judy sees in Joyce Junkin's eyes that the news has already spread.

"How you doing, Judy?"

"Well you know, Joyce, it's happened. Now, we'll just carry on and get on with it. Can you put her on the prayer chain, please?" She knocks on Bentley's door. He calls her to come in, and they sit down in the quiet of his office. With his full attention on her, she shares her self-doubts. Self-doubts are rare for her, Bentley knows. Her strategy has always been business as usual, life goes on, and we're not going to talk about it, whether the "it" is her illness or personal worries. But she had abandoned this strategy with Julie. She had let Julie see the truth of her life, the truth of how she really felt about such personal anguishes as Cyndy, not just the face that she showed to everybody else. Now, she wonders if she did the right thing by Julie. She tells Bentley that she suspects this pregnancy is Julie's way to break free in the time-honoured fashion of many an outwardly submissive female.

"I see now I was right to have adopted my strategy. I made the mistake of breaking my rule with Julie. My life was for the family, but it created the situation that led to her pregnancy. How can she have been so stupid?" Judy vacillates between fury at Julie and guilt over burdening her daughter. She agonizes that the very thing keeping her alive may have led to this, just as it had led to Cyndy running away and Miriam leaving home. Bentley lets her vent until, with a deep sigh, Judy stops speaking. She feels unburdened and ready to go on with life, just like she did after Cliff's stroke and her TPN.

She leaves to visit Julie, determined to organize Julie's house so it will be ready for the baby. Julie has a dog, cat, and boyfriend living with her in a house that looks more like a summer cottage. Judy tells her daughter that she will drive her to the obstetrician in Peterborough, that she'll take her shopping for baby clothes and all the things that she will need from diapers to a crib, and that she'll hold a shower for her later.

Baby April arrives in January 1982, and Julie and Gord marry in May, much to Judy's relief. But Cliff maintains his silence. He refuses to speak to Julie. Thinking about her father's tendency to bottle everything up, Julie decides that the best way to help them communicate again is to drop in on him at work just to say hello and chat long enough to show him that she's fine and that her life is stable. It takes a year, but he thaws and eventually accompanies Judy to coo over his first grandchild and then, in successive years, over his second and third grandchildren, Tara and Jeremy.

Meanwhile, Miriam graduates high school and enters Laurentian University. On her weekend visits to her parents' home, she jokes about how it would be nice for her dad to give her tuition money, but she pays her own way and doesn't expect anything else. She's determined to succeed on her own. From the time he had left home at sixteen to work, Cliff paid for everything with cash, except for the house in Scarborough. He had drummed this lesson into all three of his daughters. Instead of handing her money, Judy makes up regular care packages for her and tells Miriam to help herself to anything she needs in the house. Miriam appreciates her mom's efforts and believes that she has none of her own money to offer anyway.

But when Judy's mother had died, Judy had come into a nice inheritance. She told Bentley with pride that she now had her own money, money she didn't have to ask Cliff for. But she has no desire to spend it. Maintaining her life costs a lot, even though Cliff had fought the government back in 1971 for funds to cover the costs of her TPN, without having to go on welfare in order to get it, and had won. Since his stroke, they worry separately that he'll die before she does. While she feeds him enormous, nutritious muffins and skinless chicken, he squirrels money away so that when he dies she will be able to continue to live the life she's accustomed to—not a life of material wealth, but life period. He wants her to have enough money to meet her needs worry free and to help others.

Miriam completes her undergraduate degree in physical and health education in only three-and-a-half years. Judy and Cliff attend her convocation. Judy cries with happiness not only at seeing one of her daughters graduating university, but also knowing that she has been accepted to the University of Toronto's teacher college. She looks forward to the next graduation, a bit of good news in what is turning out to be a deteriorating decade. During the 1980s, Judy has given up some of her volunteer activities, but has become a literacy tutor, a less strenuous task that still allows her to help others. She feels compassion for the adults who cannot read or write and is passionate about giving them those skills. She does not see Miriam's news coming.

Miriam had met her boyfriend through work while still in her teens, and he was twenty years her senior and married. Judy used to bake Nanaimo bars and marshmallow squares for this man to sell in his restaurant, but she didn't know that he was Miriam's boyfriend. After many years of surreptitious dating, keeping the relationship from the prying ears of Bobcaygeons, this man has now left his wife, and Miriam feels free to tell her parents. Cliff is furious, but by this time, Judy can only muster "Oh, Miriam." Still, despite her disappointment, she cannot imagine what this man has in store for her daughter.

On the very last day of teacher's college, Miriam's boyfriend commits suicide. She cannot write the final exam. But the college, feeling her devastation, graduates her. She stays in Toronto to find a job. Judy understands, but tries to hold on to one last thread of control. She cannot call her daughters in Toronto because Cliff would see the long-distance calls listed on the phone bill and become upset. Instead, she has Miriam, like Cyndy, call her. And she will call them whenever she is in the hospital. That will have to do.

Chapter 23

Death Creeps Close

Judy compartmentalizes her life as a way of coping. In one compartment is her family; in another is her Bobcaygeon life; in still another is her TPN-related health problems. She doesn't like one compartment affecting any of the others. But she isn't always successful in keeping her health compartment from bleeding into the other compartments.

When Judy hears her friend has a cold on a warm January day in 1980, she decides not to stop by as had been planned. Her friend understands as the town knows that she must steer clear of infections. They can kill her. Judy doesn't like this bowing to her health needs—it puts a cramp in her social life—but it can't be helped.

March is a month of wildly fluctuating temperatures, and snow falls steadily. April showers bring temperatures in the teens, warm for this area, and an infection for Judy. She vomits. Pain flares in her muscles and joints. Chills and fever chase each other over her body, and Cliff nips into Barb Kelly's place at 8:00 AM on his way to work.

"Barb," he requests, "just check on Judy in a couple of hours to see how she is. She's got just a wee bit of a temperature. Nothing much."

Barb doesn't wait a couple of hours. She knocks on Judy's front door, opens it a crack, and calls out. She hears a moan. She opens the door fully and hastens in. She finds Judy lying on the couch, clutching her chest, moaning with pain. She places her hand on Judy's forehead. It's warm.

"Where's your thermometer, Judy?"

Judy tells her. She finds it, sticks it under Judy's tongue, and waits an interminable minute. After removing the thermometer, Barb frowns and goes over to the telephone.

"Cliff, you've got to come home. Judy's sick. Her temperature's up to ninety-nine or one hundred."

"I'm coming," he tells her. He appoints someone to manage the lumber store and heads home. As he drives, he considers calling CFB Trenton, but figures they won't get to her fast enough. Then he considers calling an ambulance. But they'll take her to the local hospital, where he'll waste time filling out paperwork and waste breath trying to explain to them what a TPN patient is and why she must go to Toronto immediately. He figures they won't listen to him because, in experts' minds, the average Joe doesn't know anything. Judy would die waiting for them to understand her predicament. He'll drive her himself. He just hopes no cop stops him for speeding.

He wheels into the driveway, hurries in, packs up her stuff, helps her out to the car, belts her in, and accelerates out of the driveway toward the 401 and TGH.

He parks in the familiar parking lot, right in front of the doors, and looks over at his wife. Judy is out cold. He zips into the hospital entrance to find a wheelchair, and when he returns, she's conscious but delirious. He coaxes her into the chair, and he speeds her along the wide hallway toward Jeej's office. It's almost 11:00 AM.

"Jeej, I've got trouble," he says as Jeej comes out of his office at his secretary's urgent summons.

Jeej looks at Judy and exclaims, "My God!" He snaps to his secretary, "Get Marlene. And page the resident on call. We have to get her to the ward now." He and Cliff push her the short distance to the nurses' station, and the nurses quickly admit her into the room right across from the station. Jeej asks Cliff if Judy has aspirated anything. Cliff doesn't know, and Judy cannot give a coherent answer. He tells Cliff that they're going to keep her in.

Judy hears her doctor and wills herself to speak. She tells Cliff to go home, knowing that's where he'd rather be, working at the lumber store and waiting for her call to say that she's better.

Marlene arrives. She's recently been promoted to TPN nurse, officially the Clinical Co-ordinator, Parenteral and Enteral Nutrition Program. She takes Judy's vitals. Her temperature has shot up to thirty-nine degrees Celsius.[1] Her blood pressure has plummeted to 95/55 mm Hg.

Jeej examines her and pronounces her "extremely sick, delirious, and toxic." Blue suffuses her mucous membranes. Her bronchia are bleeding into the airway,

---

1. The hospital switched to the metric system when Prime Minister Pierre Trudeau made it the official measuring system of Canada in the mid-1970s. The metric system is a base-ten system and is more accurate and simpler than the Imperial system of measurement.

the base of her left lung feels consolidated, her breath crackles. Yet her G-tube is draining well, and her abdomen is fine. He tells his resident to put her on tobramycin, penicillin, and cephosporin. He leaves, and Marlene stays to direct the nursing care.

Judy's cough is not productive, and they need to make it so. At first, they try chest physiotherapy. Marlene explains her plan to Judy. Judy is not keen. She fights the nurses as they pull down her blanket and then the top of her hospital gown in order to clap her chest. The hard thumps hurt her ribs, and she cannot stand more pain in her chest. With each clap, she coughs against her will until finally she spews out a green and bloody plug and then another. She breathes a little easier, but only for a moment.

Judy sinks further into delirium then into semi-consciousness. She moves erratically at irritants and picks and pulls at her TPN line, her G-tube, everything. The nurses put mitts on her hands, and Marlene realizes that chest physiotherapy has become impossible to perform. They have to suction her.

She tells Judy, who lashes out. Hoping her tone and logic will calm her down, Marlene explains in her soft voice that they have to suction her in order to make her better. Judy doesn't agree. Marlene goes ahead, though.

She directs her nurses to hold Judy's limbs down as another nurse sticks a big tube up her nose and rams it down the back of her throat and down into her lungs. They use air suction to pull out the killer secretions. It irritates her nose and makes her lungs feel like they're being turned inside out. She strains hard against the holds. Marlene worries that deep down in her memory, Judy associates being held down with cats flying out of the ceiling toward her, a hallucination from the early days of 1970 when she was also tied to the bed. She had told Marlene many years later about this terrifying hallucination.

"Stop!" Marlene commands. The nurse pulls out the suction device, and the others let go of Judy's limbs. Judy grows quiet. After a few minutes of calm, Marlene explains again to Judy that they have to do this procedure, that the secretions have to come out. They restart.

News of Judy's distress spreads throughout the hospital, and George wonders if the pharmacy had played any part in her acute infection. Were our solutions clean? He reviews the pharmacy protocols. After being part of keeping Judy alive all these years, he, like Jeej and Marlene and Judy's TPN friends, cannot accept her dying, particularly if he had contributed to her death. (He had not.)

Jeej keeps in constant touch with Marlene and comes along to check up on her whenever he can. Marlene fears that they will lose her. Jeej doesn't speak his fear out loud, and as the two watch her from the doorway, they discuss the possibility of sending her to respiratory ICU. Her lungs cannot expand properly, and if they grow even more solid, they will not oxygenate her bloodstream, and she may need a ventilator to breathe for her. Not yet, they decide.

After four days of touch-and-go, Judy improves. Her spirit and the entire staff's coordinated care have beaten death again. She opens her eyes, and they are clear. She calls Cliff, knowing exactly where he'll be, to tell her that she's fine. He'd been worrying and wondering for days and is relieved to hear her voice. They restart her TPN. As the blue recedes from her lips, yellow appears. The sepsis probably caused her jaundice, and it, too, gradually disappears. As soon as she can sit up without feeling dizzy, she heads out of her room to make her regular rounds. She wheels her pole to other rooms on the ward, spending the rest of her two-week stay gossiping with old friends and telling new "lifeliners" that their situation is no big deal and asking them to look at how well she's doing and to celebrate being alive. She visits the chapel on Sunday.

Jeej discharges her with instructions to the pharmacy to increase her calories from 1,800 to 2,300 and to add daily vitamin A. He notices xanthelasma and decides to look into cholesterol-free Liposyn as an alternative to Intralipid, which contains some cholesterol. (In the end, he decides against it.) Judy brings his attention to dryness in her vagina and asks him to have her endocrine function tested. He obeys.

Back at home, she happily slips back into her usual routine. But ill health stalks her still. Weals of red erupt on her skin for a couple of days. Then the gentamycin she's using makes her unsteady. And finally, she complains to Jeej that she has a urinary tract infection. At the hospital, he takes a culture and suggests that she go on ampicillin, depending on the results of the culturing. He dictates a long letter to Da Costa on May 9, 1980, relating this entire story. Judy does not speak this knowledge to anyone, but she knows her time of good health is over.

Chapter 24

Sweden

"Marlene, I think I'm developing an abscess near my gastrostomy tube. Do you think you can get me some Xylocaine and pack it with your stuff so that I have it for when I'm away?"

"Judy, just how bad is this?" Marlene's voice over the phone is calm, but she's having a fit at the thought of flying to Sweden with Judy suffering from an abscess.

"Oh no. It's routine ... the usual thing." The usual thing is that pain pops up underneath the skin around her G-tube hole, local cells die, pus collects, and huge numbers of white cells rush in, inflaming the skin into a nice red hill around the black hole, until the abscess breaks, and it all oozes out.

Judy had said yes to going to the Gastroenterological World Congress in Stockholm from June 12–18, 1982, only if someone would go with her. Marlene had volunteered. With seats booked and medical clearances completed successfully, Judy and Marlene are ready to fly.

The flight attendant settles them into their seats. Aware that the plane's refrigerator contains important items for Judy, she hovers nearby whenever she can. Dinnertime arrives, and Judy says no to food. This puzzles the flight attendant. Judy refuses all drinks, except water, from the cart as well. The flight attendant is not happy. As they approach the eastern side of the Atlantic Ocean, again Judy refuses food, which brings a frown to the flight attendant's face. She comes by again with the drinks cart to try and entice her and worries when Judy continues to say no. It's a long flight. Judy must eat something, anything.

With each pass of the cart, she fusses more until finally Judy says, "Well, I don't eat."

The flight attendant raises her eyebrows and looks closely at her. The woman hasn't been drinking, but ... Her thought trails off, and she moves on, but returns quickly, sits down near this mysterious woman, and asks about this not-eating business. Judy tells her. The flight attendant is enthralled.

But she is no more enthralled than Ingalill Bergqvist, International Product Manager for Intralipid, which is manufactured by KabiVitrum, the sponsors of the congress. She greets Judy and Marlene at Arlanda Stockholm Airport on Sunday, June 13, soon after they disembark at 9:30 in the morning. She's pleased that she recognizes Judy. She whisks them to Hotel Malmen, apologizing several times about having forgotten to bring Judy an IV pole. (Judy had to leave Lester behind.) But no matter, Judy and Marlene commandeer a coat rack from the hotel.

Judy rests before learning that she's to do a taped radio interview that day.

That night, she and Marlene get a hotel staff person to accompany them to the kitchen, which is closing for the day, to retrieve Judy's solutions from the fridge where the hotel manager had put them. A heavy-set woman stops them as they barrel through the kitchen door. She won't let them get to the fridge. She is in charge, and the kitchen is closed. To make matters worse, her English is poor, they speak no Swedish, and the subject matter is unbelievable.

"We need to get into the refrigerator for her food," Marlene explains.

"No, no, no, not serving food."

"Not *food* food, but *solutions* food."

"Not serving food."

They go back and forth until finally the heavy-set woman throws out an arm toward the fridge in surrender. Marlene opens the refrigerator door and fishes out three TPN solution bags. The woman's eyes widen, and she throws up her hands and exclaims, "Why, I don't know, I don't know."

Marlene explains, "This is that lady's food."

"No, here, a sandwich."

"No. This is her food," Marlene taps one of the bags.

"No, thank you," Judy says at the same time.

"Here, a sandwich," she replies.

"No." Judy sees this back-and-forth isn't going to stop. She unbuttons her blouse and hauls out her Langer Line. The woman staggers, and Marlene reaches out to steady her.

"Oh, my dear," she says, recovering. She wraps her arms around Judy, telling her whatever she needs, just ask.

Back in their room, the door closed against everyone but Marlene, Judy doubles over and clutches at her stomach. Marlene hands her the Xylocaine for her abscess and asks, "Can I do something?"

"No," Judy breathes out. "It's just a matter of time. It will drain on its own." The Xylocaine numbs the pain. Relieved, Judy sits on her bed and looks at Marlene. "I have my own way of doing things."

"Judy, you do your thing. I'm not here to tell you how to do it."

"Well, you know, I don't always do things exactly as told."

"If you need some help, I'm here. You holler, otherwise do your thing." And with that, Marlene picks up a magazine and relaxes against the headboard of her bed.

Judy watches her for a moment before getting up to bring the coat rack closer to her bed. She starts her TPN routine.

Marlene peeks over the top of her magazine. She notices Judy doesn't wear a mask. I'm not going to criticize her, she thinks. This woman's been doing this for eons. She resumes reading.

Sharp and clear northern light filters through the curtains early, waking the two up. After breakfast, Judy asks Marlene to help her write a short summary. She feels unnerved at the idea of giving a formal talk to a room filled with doctors and nurses, but a summary she can do. However, the Swedish trip is not all work. The folks at KabiVitrum want her to see Stockholm, too. Ingalill is not always available to escort Judy and Marlene cannot be with her all the time either, as she is here to attend events at the congress as well, and so the marketing director's secretary has been tasked to take good care of Judy.

Britt Lindqvist is thrilled at being given this responsibility, as she had heard about Judy and Jeej from the day she'd started working at Vitrum AB back in the fall of 1973. Britt stays with Judy throughout much of the trip, learns to spot when she's tiring, and figures out when it's best to bypass the noisy guided tour and to go at Judy's real pace. She has planned a flexible itinerary. When she meets Judy on her first morning in Sweden, she gives her a copy and explains all that she has planned for her. But first, the media want to meet her. Britt escorts her to the Grand Hotel, where Swedish TV is waiting to interview Judy.

The boat tour to see the bridges of Stockholm is scheduled to depart at 1:00 PM. It doesn't start well. It's chilly, there's a bit of a crowd, and chaos breaks out as everyone tries to get onboard. Britt fears for Judy. Yet Judy cracks jokes, and the tension eases.

They decide to skip the visit to the National Museum of Fine Arts. Back at the hotel, beautiful roses from Wretlind greet Judy, to her delight.

Tuesday starts at 9:30 AM with a three-hour visit to Drottningholm Palace, the country home of the Swedish royal family. This is the only time Judy reveals her fragility to Britt. At the foot of the palace's grand marble staircase, she hesitates. She feels uneasy, but she wants to follow the guide. Britt suggests that she'll go up the stairs right behind Judy to cushion her if she does fall. Judy likes the idea and climbs the stairs carefully. On the way back down, Britt goes just in front of her. At the bottom, she thanks Britt. "It was marvellous to experience such places with this old history. We don't have these old buildings in Canada." Britt swells with pleasure.

Now it's time for Judy to work. They return to the city by boat, as the weather is fine. Dr. Erik Vinnars had asked Judy and Marlene to visit a young woman at the hospital who is ready to be discharged home on TPN. At the hospital, the doctors and nurses express their concerns to Marlene and Judy about how their patient will manage on her own living on an island far from the hospital.

"Well, Judy lives two hours from the hospital," Marlene informs the staff.

Their eyes open wide. "How has she managed?"

While Marlene answers this question, Judy approaches the young woman. She, too, is worried about how she'll manage. Judy tells her that she has coped for over a decade and that she's fine. The woman's fears evaporate under Judy's warm confidence. The visit ends with an interview with a newspaper reporter. The planned visit to the Milles Sculpture Garden is cancelled so that Judy can rest before the evening's celebration.

Twelve Canadians and their new friends fête this banner day at a posh hotel by the river. A waiter takes food orders, but when he approaches Judy, she tells him, "No, thank you." He frowns. He asks again. She says no again. Judy can see he's upset that she's occupying his table but not eating. He insists. She starts to feel awkward in front of all these people at perpetually having to say no.

Marlene rises, takes the waiter's arm, and pulls him away. "Excuse me, but this lady does not and medically cannot eat. And I would appreciate it if you don't pressure her any longer."

He looks over at this so-called ill lady and looks back at Marlene. He's not buying it.

"Look, we're a group of physicians. I am the nurse. And she is the patient."

He looks properly this time. Judy, watching their exchange, smiles her glorious, eye-crinkling smile, the one that pulls people in. He smiles back. He's hooked. He believes. He ensures that she's well cared for the rest of the night as the others feast on caviar, wine, reindeer, and cloudberries.

Wednesday, June 16 is Judy's big day. Throughout breakfast, her nerves ratchet up. At Mässan, the site of the congress, Jeej, Marlene, George, Wretlind, Joe Fischer, and Henri Joyeux (from France) step up to the podium for a special symposium on home parenteral nutrition. Wretlind brings out two women and asks the packed room, "Which do you think is the patient?" The attendees are perplexed. Both look healthy. Both look normal. He introduces Judy as the patient. The audience gasps and applauds wildly as she takes her place on the panel. She reads her summary, and Wretlind invites questions from the audience.

"Judy, what's it like to be on home TPN?"

Judy hesitates before averring, "It feels good."

The room roars, and Judy relaxes and enters the fray of the question-and-answer session with gusto, referring some questions to the experts on the panel and adding her own take to the occasional question directed at one of the medical people. But the experts on the panel are just the supporting cast to the star: Judy.

Wretlind ends the session so that Jeej and Judy can make their way to the press conference in room K 14. Ever since they had landed, Judy's telephone has rung with so many interview requests that Marlene has become Judy's press agent, not just her nurse. Now, those reporters fill a room, eager for their chance to talk to Judy directly.

Jeej speaks to the crowd about Judy's history and describes home TPN, the location of the Langer Line, and her feeding routine. Then he takes questions. Everyone zooms in on Judy.

"Judy, what's it like to be on home TPN?"

"Do people notice?"

"Judy, you look so well. How do you do it?"

"Where are your tubes and bags?"

"Judy, are you ever sick?"

Judy boggles at the difference between this conference and the one held a month earlier in Toronto, where—despite Marlene's persistent calling of the press—only a *Toronto Star* reporter showed up. The reporter had written up a tiny article on what was happening with home TPN in Canada. Here in Sweden, the jostling journalists are rabid to know everything until Jeej calls a halt to the Q&A. Judy has started to tire, and he has other commitments at the congress.

The marketing department hosts a luncheon at 1:00 PM for Judy, Marlene, and George. Judy notices the director's unease at her drinking only water at a luncheon in her honour, and so she starts joking with them all. Her enthusiasm infects the others, and the room fills with chatter as food fills their stomachs. Judy takes note of what they are eating and records it in her itinerary: "Delicious—shrimp, steak."

Britt calls for Judy that evening at her hotel to take her on the four-hour Archipelago Tour, which starts at the quay outside the Grand Hotel at 7:00 PM under the bright northern sun. Judy enjoys it hugely and finds it very much like her familiar stomping grounds of the Haliburton Waterways, where she and Cliff sometimes boat during the summer. (She no longer has a fear of getting wet, having gained confidence about what she can and cannot do from her decade of experience on TPN.) Again, food plays a part in the itinerary, and Judy eagerly sops it all up into her memory. By this time, Britt is getting used to eating in front of Judy, whether it's raw or smoked herring or strawberries and cream. But even those who know Judy well can feel uneasy eating around her and don't realize how much vicarious pleasure she takes from watching them consume food, as Marlene is learning on this trip.

After spending Thursday morning together sightseeing (Judy had the luxury of sleeping in first) and shopping for T-shirts, Marlene's stomach starts to rumble. Judy looks at her. "Okay, it's lunchtime. You have to eat."

"Oh no, it's okay."

"No, no, no, you have to eat. Just 'cause I don't eat, doesn't mean you can't. I eat all night; you don't. So it's time for your lunch. Let's go get lunch." She drags Marlene to an enticing restaurant, looks over Marlene's menu, and points out what she should eat, ending with dessert. "I think you should have some cloudberry ice cream." Marlene duly orders the dessert, and they share. Judy puts a spoonful in her mouth. She closes her lips over the spoon bowl, enjoying the feel of the cold dessert on her palate. She pulls the utensil out slowly as she lets the ice cream melt in her mouth, the flavour exploding her taste buds. She exclaims as the cold cream flows out her G-tube into her leg bag, freezing her leg, but the deliciousness of the ice cream is worth the hit of cold, and she laughs it off. Anyway, this happens often when she drinks cold water, which is so refreshing in her mouth. Marlene has not seen this side of being on home TPN before and files it away in her mind to help her patients back at home.

Finally that night, Judy has supper with Jeej, and the next day she "Shopped!!!" and "Walked!!!" to her heart's content, as she scrawls on her itinerary.

Ingalill and her daughter Anna take Judy and Marlene on a final sightseeing tour to Skansen, the open-air museum. Judy's abscess has not yet broken and drained, and the pain threatens to overwhelm her. But when she hears that the Bergqvists have two dachshunds, she gets them talking about dogs, theirs and hers, soaking up every detail so that her mind has no room for the pain.

By the end of the week, Britt and Judy are friends. She invites Judy and her gang to her home for a casserole dinner on the last night of their stay. They enjoy a pleasant evening in Britt's apartment. Judy sits on the couch, looking out the window at the late-night sun and the view of the lake, memorizing this moment.

The abscess is a distant memory. The pain is gone. This dinner with her hosts and her health-care team, this week of seeing another country and another culture, this time of being in demand, this moment is reality. I am a lucky girl, she thinks.

Chapter 25

Breaking Bones,
Falling Hair

Judy's luck, though she is not aware of it as she sits at Britt's window, had started to worsen awhile ago in July of 1976.

She had sprained her wrist on July 3 and then fell on her knee on July 26, 1976. That made her walk stiffly for awhile, but she brushed it off.

Jeej did not brush it off when he saw her during a regular appointment and asked about her stiff gait. "Judy, I want you to have a bone biopsy. It will be a bit uncomfortable," he told her.

"You mean it will hurt like hell," she retorted.

Jeej smiled to concede the point. He said his secretary would book the appointment.

Rain poured down on Monday, March 28, 1977. Rather appropriate, Judy thought as she waited for the bone guy, as Jeej had called him. He rushed into the room and before she was ready had her up on a table, her back to him, and was telling her to relax and that it will only be a pinprick. She stayed still with fear.

He injected a local anaesthetic over the iliac crest part of the pelvis. Judy felt the familiar prick and then the familiar fatter and fatter feeling of numbness. He pressed her flesh, and when she could not feel his finger, he started. She didn't feel pain as the slender needle punctured her skin, slid through her fat and muscle, and hit the bone. He whirled the needle into the bone through to her marrow. She gasped. She tried to breathe against the pain. It was over. He had his bone core. She checked that the needle was really out and rubbed the insulted area, willing the pain to recede. Within a few minutes, she got up and walked out.

She finally saw Jeej in July to learn the results. She sat down across from him at his desk, nervous about what he was going to tell her.

"Your biopsy shows markedly reduced bone mass and a hyperkinetic bone turnover with increase in osteoid seam and resorption sites. I was afraid of this. What it means is this. Vitamin D increases calcium absorption. The blood calcium levels rise. And when the blood calcium levels rise consistently, it shuts off the parathyroid hormone. And when the parathyroid hormone shuts off, it stops the turnover, or remodelling, of bone. And the bone crumbles."

Judy cringed inwardly.

"So when we reduced your vitamin D, we reduced the absorption of calcium. And because you are reducing the absorption of calcium, you're actually reducing blood calcium levels. And when blood calcium levels fall, then parathyroid hormone starts to be secreted. And that increases the remodelling of bone.

"Now before we removed the vitamin D from your alimentation, you might have developed osteomalacia. And by taking away the vitamin D, we healed it. The problem is that the bone that had formed in that period without calcium got reabsorbed and then calcified. So you are left only with the original, thin piece."

Judy watched his lips, unblinking.

"You see, bone formation is a very complex issue. It's easy to stop the breakdown of bone, but it's very difficult to increase the mass of bone, particularly once you're beyond 30 years of age. And you're how old?"

"Forty-one," she reminded him.

"So you see, your bones may have become brittle. You haven't had any fractures yet?"

"No, just bruises."

"Good. I don't like you falling so much. But by taking out the vitamin D and giving you more calcium etc., I'm hoping that will help matters. But, you know, we have no idea what is going on. This is all new."

Judy nodded. This is all new. We don't know. How many times had she heard those phrases before? They'd given her life, though. She could not think of a question to ask and so left worried. But as one year slipped into the next and as her bones remained unbroken, she stopped worrying.

Clouds gathered on the morning of Tuesday, June 5, 1979, and poured out their tears before moving on that evening, but not before Judy fell twice, the second time while shopping at Knob Hills, a large supermarket, with her neighbour Cathy. Her wrist swelled and blared its pain. Cathy drove her home quickly, and Judy called her GP Da Costa.

Judy arrived at his empty office after hours. He examined her wrist and was pretty sure that it was broken. He wrapped an old copy of *Time* magazine tightly round it and taped it in place. He then injected her with 75 mg of Demerol to hold the pain at bay until the next morning when she could go to the fracture clinic at the Lindsay Hospital. It was closed at night. She joked that the magazine will be mighty handy to read. Neither spoke about how often she falls.

She showed Jeej her cast during her next appointment, which happened to be just before he left for his annual August vacation. She asked him, "How long should this cast be on?"

"About three weeks. Why? How long has it been on?"

"Since June 6."

"Oh." He put his hand up to his mouth and thought about that for a minute. "And how did you break it?"

"I fell in Knob Hills. I saved my knee but broke my wrist." She tried to hide her worry.

"This isn't the first time you've fallen?"

"No."

"It's your first fracture, though?"

"Yes."

Jeej opened her chart. He paid particular attention to her vitamin D–related blood-test results. He flipped backward through the chart and saw that in 1974 he had cut Judy's vitamin D in half because her serum magnesium was down and her serum phosphorus was up, the latter a problem that had started to appear in his other TPN patients as well. Subsequently, he had worked with George to combine vitamin A in another preparation so that he could take vitamin D out of the TPN altogether, instead of just halving it as he had originally done with Judy. But as he had feared, the damage had been done.

Judy interrupted his thoughts, "I'm wondering if I should come to Toronto to have my cast removed in case I have metabolic bone disease. Is that why I'm healing slowly?"

"I don't know. I think you should have an X-ray. Then we'll see."

Judy headed down to X-ray and soon returned with film in hand. Jeej placed it up onto his light box, and they looked at it together.

"Well," he said, "it shows good position and satisfactory progress. I don't think you need worry. You can go to your local hospital to have it removed."

"Are you sure?"

"Yes, I'm sure."

Judy left with requisitions for more blood tests, worrying that this fracture was a harbinger of new problems to cope with. Ever since Jeej had cured her diabetes, her days had been full. She'd focused her attention on her friends and family, serving others, helping her fellow lifeliners, and volunteering at her church. She'd ignored the abscess, bleeding gums, and abundant scale on her teeth until she had no choice but to deal with them. She'd willed out of her mind the inconveniences from being on TPN and the bruises from her falls. But now the bruise had become a broken bone.

The heavy cast, its unyielding presence, reminded her that being the first person on home TPN held a price. She was grateful that Jeej had caught the toxic levels of too much vitamin D early; it could've been so much worse, she reminded herself as she swallowed her distress about breaking more bones and losing her independence. This was just another part of her illness. And at this point, she had yet to see any grandchildren. She must not die before reaching that goal. And she could not become that predicted quasi-invalid after all these years. Heck, she was so close to the ten-year mark that she could not let this get her down. Jeej would find a cure, just as he had before. She squared her shoulders and headed for the blood lab.

It's fall 1982, the trip to Sweden a sweet, lingering memory. The leaves falling off the trees mimic the fine hair falling out of Judy's head. Like every woman, she likes her hair to look decent, and this new problem is too much.

"I'm losing a lot of hair, Jeej," she announces on October 18, 1982. "What are you going to do about it?"

Jeej studies her head after he examines her line and her G-tube. "I would say you have somewhat thin hair. But what concerns me is that your G-tube is clearly very excoriated."

"I know." Judy doesn't like to be reminded of this never-ending problem. Having to deal with it twice a day is bad enough.

"I suggest you try to lift the tube off your skin and protect it with a mixture of zinc and cod liver oil."

"Well, I'd rather put it on me than eat it!" she jokes to Jeej, referring to the oil. Maybe, she thinks, this will finally stop her stomach juices from eating her skin. "I'll try."

"Good."

"What about my hair?"

"Don't worry about it."

She doesn't; she just hates losing it. In one breath, she continues to complain about it whenever she visits Da Costa or Jeej or the friendly young physicians at the Home TPN Clinic that Jeej has set up in the new Eaton Wing on the ninth floor. In the next breath, she shrugs her shoulders and asserts it's just part of the illness. Still, she hopes one of the doctors will come up with a solution. Finally, the young residents at the Home TPN Clinic on a freezing January day respond to her persistence. They add biotin in the form of Berocca-C to her TPN. Much to her delight, her hair grows back—unfortunately, only temporarily.

By October 1986, strands of hair are falling all over the bathroom counter, kitchen table, the back of her chair, her pillow. She's constantly picking or vacuuming it up and throwing it out. She pesters Jeej about it again, and he increases her Berocca-C, hoping that will solve her problem so that he can concentrate on fixing her G-tube leaks and brittle bones. She hasn't thought about the latter in a long time because, once again, years of no breaks have lulled her into complacency, and unlike some of the other lifeliners, she has no bone pain to remind her of the creeping destruction within. She prefers not to think about unpleasant things. She just feels so grateful to be alive and to have Cliff at her side. She shares her feelings with Cliff by handing him an article to read in the *LifelineLetter* from the Oley Foundation. He scans the headline, "Are You a Caregiver?" He pauses and looks up briefly, but she says nothing and continues to knit. He silently reads the rest of the short article: "If so, you may need to pay more attention to your own health care needs, according to an article in the *American College of Physicians' Observer.*" It continues: "Known as the 'loneliest job in town' or the '36-hour day,' the physical and emotional health of caregivers can often be taxed to the limit." When he finishes reading, he hands the article back to her with a nod. She puts it in a box with her other keepsakes. Life goes on.

Chapter 26

LifelineLetter Award

Judy, Sandra Lapenny (her former camp charge and now fast friend and fellow lifeliner), Sandra Lacey, and a couple other members of the year-old Canadian TPN Patient Association, as they formally call themselves, arrive in Saratoga Springs, New York, on a lovely but hot July day in 1987. The American Oley Foundation has held annual picnics for four years and conferences for two, and the Canadians have attended a few of them. This year is a special one, for Judy is the first recipient of the award Oley has just set up, and the foundation is paying for Judy's travel expenses as the monetary portion of the award.

On the first night of the conference, the American hosts invite all the participants to dinner at the Wishing Well, a local restaurant. Don Young, one of the organizers and a lifeliner himself, had already spoken to the owner about the differing food requirements and had explained that he wasn't even sure how many people would turn up. Twenty gather round a table. Judy and Sandra sit across from each other. A waitress with white, permed hair broaches the noisy group to take their orders one by one. She comes to Sandra and asks what she would like. Sandra looks across the table at Judy and asks her, "Are you going to buy my dinner tonight?"

"No, I'm not. I'm not buying your dinner tonight. That's it," Judy asserts.

Sandra looks up at the waitress and says, "No, I can't have anything. I don't have any money."

"Oh, all right. I'll buy you a cup of tea," Judy sighs. "You can have that."

"Okay, I'll have that," Sandra says as she hands the menu to the appalled waitress.

"Sandra, I'll buy you dinner," one of the sweet Americans offers.

"No, no, that's all right."

"Here, take the menu and buy whatever it is you want."

"She's not eating," Judy announces.

The group freezes, not knowing what to say, caught between Sandra's plight and Judy's implacability. Sandra and Judy crack up, throwing their heads back and howling with laughter. Like Judy and unlike most people on home TPN, Sandra cannot eat any food, for she, too, has no bowels left. Smiles break out, and the waitress relaxes and moves on to the next customer. The dinner goes late into the night, the crowd moving from the table to gather around the piano to sing. Judy's voice soars above all others.

On Saturday, the Canadians cannot wait for the picnic and head out early, arriving well before the 11:00 AM start time. The Americans have the same idea. They descend on the back lawn of St. Joseph's Catholic Church at Greenfield Center. Judy does not remain incognito for long. So many know her voice from their phone calls to her seeking help and encouragement or know her face from medical journals and newspaper articles, and they cannot wait to speak to her in person, touch her, feel her presence. As one lifeliner says to another, "If Judy can be out here doing all these things, I've got to at least talk to her." Each has his or her turn to say hello, ask a question or three, and just listen. Judy ignores no one. And as everyone finishes their moments with her, they turn to their friends and exclaim, "Wow! This woman is so dynamic! She has so much energy."

Don walks over to the tent, puts his hands up to his mouth, and calls for everyone's attention. He eventually penetrates the excited din surrounding Judy, and he calls her to join him under the tent. The acolytes part to let Judy through. Dr. Lyn Howard and Clarence Oldenburg join Don and Judy, Clarence looking sharp in his straw hat and the two women looking cool in their summery dresses on this hot day. Howard moves to one side of Judy, Clarence to the other. Don steps away.

Howard starts telling the story of Judy, while Clarence watches Judy with affection, and Judy finds the fresh green grass a good view. The crowd barely rustles, not wanting to miss a detail. Howard stops speaking and picks up a framed certificate from the table nearby. Judy looks up.

"I'm proud to present to Judy Taylor the very first LifelineLetter Award, on behalf of the Oley Foundation. We have set up this award for an adult HPEN consumer—or caregiver—who has been on therapy for at least five years and has demonstrated courage, perseverance, a positive attitude in dealing with illness, and exceptional generosity in helping others in their struggle with Home PEN. We wish to thank David Holder [an early homecare-company executive] for making this award possible. Judy is the obvious and unanimous choice of us all."

Judy accepts the certificate and looks at it as the crowd of 150 claps and whistles its approval.

"Thank you." Judy looks at her certificate again and then back up at the crowd. "I love you for giving me this award. I'm very, very thrilled for this, but it's other people that have got me here, you know. My family had to sacrifice for me. Dr. Jeejeebhoy gave me back my life." Judy stops and blinks hard. She cannot continue. One by one, they clap into a thunder. When it's over and people have started to mingle again, the conference's unofficial official photographer asks the three to pose together. *Click. Click.* Just one more, he asks. *Click.* Judy loosens, looks around, and disappears into her mob of groupies.

Back at home, Judy relives that high many times as June becomes summer and summer cools into fall. On the night of Thursday, September 10, 1987, she turns over in bed and cracks a right rib. She inhales sharply. Her heart accelerates. Adrenaline races through her. Thoughts of how others sneeze and break a vertebrae flood her mind. Da Costa bandages her up, and Jeej continues to work at finding a cure. But her bones no longer hide their insult. Ribs fracture, an arm breaks, and bandages and casts appear on her body over the waning years of the 1980s. Slowly, reluctantly, she realizes that, although Jeej has found a cure for everything else, he will not be able to cure her bones or her G-tube. It's just a matter of time now. She and Cliff talk about how many years they think she has left. They think five. She has reached her goal of seeing her grandkids born. She has watched them start to grow up, she takes them to church every Sunday, and she revels in being Nana to Julie's three children.

She tells Susan Clayton, her neighbour, during one of their frequent visits, "You know, you've got to live through today, not yesterday and not tomorrow, but just through today. You've got to get through today, or you're not going to see tomorrow." She breathes in deeply and exhales gratitude for her life. "Susan," she says, "stop and take time to look around. Enjoy your life to the fullest; don't take anything for granted. Like, if a bird is going by, take a look at it. You know, it might be a rare bird that you haven't seen before. Take time to work in your garden and take the beauty out of the flowers." Judy loves roses and pauses as she envisions her favourite flower. "You know, take a look at your trees and stuff like that. There are so many simple things in life people take for granted, and it's all part of life. But most people are just in the fast lane and go, go, go, and they miss, they miss 90 percent of their life. You live your life to the fullest."

Judy talks to her about death as well, especially since Susan is dealing with much sickness and the death of her grandmother. "Well, you're not really dying. You're just going to a better place. If we're suffering here, the afterlife is going to be much better. You have to look at it that way." The glow of goodness that always radiates from Judy and her matter-of-fact words bring peace to Susan.

Although Judy feels content with what Jeej has given her, she's determined to enjoy every moment left to her. For Judy, Oley conferences are must-attend events. She plans her annual trips down to the last detail.

Judy writes on cream notepaper with a bunch of fall flowers decorating the bottom left:

May 18/88

Hi Jeej,

This is just a note to ask if you will send me another letter clearing my solutions, etc for crossing the border. Eight of us are off to the Oley Conference and as they are getting pretty sticky about drugs at the U.S. border I'd rather not have to use last years letter.

Thanks for the trouble.

Judy Taylor.

She makes Sandra Lapenny her permanent roommate, and although Sandra's husband would like to attend, Sandra and her husband both know that these four or five days every year at the Oley conference are special to Judy. Judy and Sandra go everywhere together when they're in Saratoga Springs, except for the one night Sandra decides to go to an Irish bar and Judy reneges on the plans, being too tired. Before she leaves, Sandra asks which of the two books Judy brought will be on her reading agenda that night: her smutty reading or the Bible. Judy grins. It's Harlequin tonight. Sandra returns at an early hour and falls into bed after hooking up her own TPN.

Bang. Bang. Bang. "Get out of here! Get out of here now!" The fire alarm shrills through the hotel. Judy leaps out of bed, yelling at Sandra. "Get up, get up! There's a fire!"

Judy hurries out, nightgown flapping, pushing Lester, her hair sticking up, down, and sideways. Sandra is close behind, but can't stop thinking about losing her possessions and runs back for her favourite Blue Jays sweatshirt. She exits last out the hotel door and into the parking lot and stops. Her jaw drops. Laughter bubbles out uncontrollably.

"What is so funny?" Judy demands.

"Judy, if you could just see yourself. Your hair is sticking straight up, you've got only your nightgown on, and you're tied to Lester." She doubles over laughing. Judy smiles, but is distracted by hearing the fire door open. Firefighters straggle out and halt bemused when they see the parking-lot party of patients with their forest of poles and pumps and their nightclothes riffling in the breeze at one o'clock in the morning. The only one all dressed and made up, with earrings on, is Marlene.

"You can go back in now," the captain tells them. "It's safe." The firefighters try not to stare while the group files past them with poles on wheels, lights flashing on the pumps, and tubes disappearing down their tops. Judy loves every silly and learning moment of the Oley conferences, even when she is part of the learning moments for others, as is the case on Friday, June 23, 1989, when she is the first speaker at the conference.

With a few presentations now under her belt, Judy is more excited about travelling with her friends than nervous about the speech itself. She has tasked Sandra Lapenny to be her slide-projector operator, and Sandra obediently has practised until perfect. Judy will not put up with flubs, she knows.

"Good morning, everyone. Just want to warn you that any strange noises from up here are my knees knocking."

It's the next morning. Judy has just stepped up to the microphone. The packed room erupts in laughter, and she relaxes.

"Having been asked to speak on where we were in TPN, I'll try to tell you of my beginnings, as well as what some other programs were doing in the early seventies.

"First, the technical aspects. While in hospital, dressings were easy. A trip down the hall to the utility room to pick up a sterilized dressing tray, back to my room, and so to work. Upon going home, things were very different. We had to sterilize our own trays."

She checks the screen to see if Sandra has the first slide up. She does.

"This involved putting a large ..." She flips to the next handwritten page of her speech. "... roasting pan filled with water, a metal dressing tray, forceps, etc. on the stove and boiling it all for 15 minutes." She glances toward Sandra, as Sandra prepares to click the slide projector button for the next slide. "When cooled, the necessary supplies, gauze, tape, iodine, alcohol, etc. were added, and we did our dressing. In those days, (next slide Sandra) a daily gauze dressing was done, not like today when we use disposable trays and op-sites.

"With respect to my feedings, see the next slide, we have always had our amino acid, dextrose in plastic bags, as opposed to bottles. Initially, I had three separate bags, but now I have a single bag containing three litres. I only had to add vitamins and my own medications. This, I realize, was different from some other centres where patients received bottles of solutions that they had to mix together along with all the additives. Lipids were a part of my daily diet in hospital from the beginning in 1970, as you can see from the next slide. This was infused by gravity over four hours. I understand that this, too, was different from here in the U.S., where lipids were not available until the late seventies.

"By mid-1970, we were delivering our two or three litres of amino acid, dextrose solutions through a pneumatic infusion device." Sandra changes the slide. "It consisted of a compressed-air cylinder attached to a red regulator, which controlled the air being released into three pressure bags containing the bags of solution. The bags of solution were connected in series. The air pressure ensured a constant flow, and the drip rate was controlled by a roller clamp. All this paraphernalia hung from an IV pole. When my pole was presented to me, meaning I could at last go home, it came already christened with the name Lester and eyes and a smiling mouth painted on the pressure bags."

Laughter interrupts her. She waits until it dies down and continues.

"This infusion ran for twelve to fourteen hours, overnight. At this point in time, overnight infusions were not common. Many patients received their solutions twenty-four hours a day. For this reason, various ambulatory devices were invented. For example, you can see on the next slide that Scandinavia used a backpack system which took either bags or bottles." She pauses as her written speech instructs and inhales deeply. She looks at Sandra, who switches to the next slide, and continues. "In France, solutions, including lipid, were placed in sausage-shaped bags, which were worn like collars around the neck with a small pump at the waist.

"I was lucky because Dr. Jeejeebhoy, realizing the psychological impact of being restricted by such an apparatus, decided that we could be disconnected in order to lead a more active life." She gestures to the screen. "Therefore, heparin was infused into the catheter. At this time, it meant taping a ten cc syringe, with or without forceps, to your chest. Really added to your body image and sex appeal."

The crowd howls, and she waits until she can be heard again.

"Now as you can see from the slides, we have a nice, little blue cap to plug in as well as extension tubes to secure the catheter wherever you see fit. That's one of the reasons for brassieres. Too bad, fellas!

"In hospital, in the beginning, on twenty-four-hour infusion, no one could explain why I felt so miserable by mid-afternoon. Upon closer scrutiny and with much giggling and guffawing, the medical diagnosis was handed down. I was hung over! It seems that one of the components of my solutions was alcohol—hence, I was getting drunk. Fortunately or unfortunately, depending on your point of view, this problem was remedied. The next first in the scientific evolution of TPN was the discovery that I was diabetic. Further investigation proved that this was not entirely true—yes, my blood sugars were elevated, and I had peripheral neuropathy, but the cause was not an insulin deficiency but rather a lack of chromium. Once this was added to my solutions, my symptoms disappeared. With all this chromium in me, they promised to polish me up for Christmas. Since then, research has been done into the need for other trace metals such as copper selenium, zinc, etc., which we all now receive.

"Finally and perhaps most important has been the change in our lifestyle. Some of this is due to technology, but much is due to a change in attitude and acceptance not only among patients, but also among health-care professionals that one *can* lead a normal and active life on home TPN. For example, when first discharged from hospital, we moved a hundred miles away into the country where I was to live the quiet life as a semi-invalid. Dr. Jeejeebhoy arranged with the emergency services to have helicopter pick-up if any problems arose. Thank heaven this never was necessary, because I'm afraid of heights and terrified of the thought of riding in a helicopter. As for a quiet life, it simply wasn't possible with three kids—seven, nine, and eleven—at home and glad to have Mom back after a ten-month absence. In addition, the cat was having kittens, and the kitchen cupboards were being constructed in the dining room. In time, I learned to drive, was teaching sewing and cooking to about fourteen teenagers in the 4-H club, looking after two horses, bowling, and occasionally having a ride on the neighbour's minibike. I was even lucky enough to have a trip to Sweden, where I spent a great but gruelling ten days touring Stockholm with some friendly locals. The original purpose of this trip was to be on a panel at an international medical conference, but it was more fun being a 'tourist' than a 'specimen.' Other patients go camping, swimming, moose hunting into the backwoods of northern Ontario, or even touring Europe.

"I hope I've given you a bit of insight into the beginnings of TPN and a few of the differences. Just remember that things keep improving as research continues and that living with Lester, or your pump or whatever, is a whole lot better than the alternative. If you have faith and a sense of humour, you are more than half-way there.

"Thank you."

Applause thunders through the room. Judy stays at the microphone, soaking it in, her smile broadening and cheeks reddening as the crowd stands up en masse, clapping enthusiastically. She floats to sleep that night.

She cannot wait until next year and ensures nothing gets in the way of her going. George has moved to Novopharm as Director of Hospital Services, and she decides to approach him for some funding to help them make the trip. Judy writes in her looping, large hand:

May 26, 1990

Mr. George Tsallas
Novopharm/LyphoMed Pharmaceutical Co.
7181 Woodbine Ave., Unit 110
Markham, Ont.
L3R 1A3

Dear George:

As you know some of us who are HPEN (Home Parenteral and Enteral Nutrition) patients try to attend the Oley Foundation Conference in Saratoga Springs every summer. We have always found this conference very informative as the speakers are well versed in their topics and of course, the opportunity to exchange ideas and do some problem solving amongst ourselves is always a learning experience. Although this will be the first year that at least one of the Toronto contingent is not either a speaker, discussion leader, or award winner, we will participate in every possible area and report back to the rest of our group at the fall meeting.

Last year your company was kind enough to assist us with the expenses involved in this endeavour and we were very grateful. I am writing to you now to ask if you would again be interested in providing financial assistance. We are going to drive as it cuts the cost of plane fare. Any help you might give would be most welcome.

Thank you again for your support last year and hope you will find it possible to do so this year. The conference is the weekend of the 13 and 14 of July.

Yours truly

Judy Taylor

She adds her phone number to the end of her letter.

George comes through with a cheque for a hundred dollars and asks her to let him know earlier next time, before all their funding commitments have been made for the year. Neither he nor she has an inkling that this 1990 trip is her last one.

Chapter 27

Dr. Cowboy, Where Are You?

"Laura, can you come over? I want to talk to you about something."

"Sure," Laura replies. Judy had met Laura Armstrong, a nurse, when she'd accompanied Laura's sister and Nancy Hill, a mutual friend, to help Laura move from Newfoundland back to Ontario. In the mid-1980s, Judy decides to change the nature of their relationship.

Judy gets right to the point as soon as Laura arrives. "I've been having trouble with my G-tube. Whenever I need it changed, my only option is to go to Toronto because I'd rather not have doctors do it. Even Jeej is no good at it. I can get the nurses to change it in Toronto when I go down once a month, but in between I need to have some option other than making a flying trip to Toronto."

"Sure, Judy, I'll do it."

"I like it done a certain way," Judy warns.

"I've never changed one of those before, so I'll do it in whatever way you show me."

Judy smiles in relief. Now when she moves improperly, shifts the G-tube, and gets it stuck in the wrong direction, she has someone to help her fix it. She tries to wait as long as possible for her first call to Laura, but finally she succumbs. She arranges for Laura to come over during the day when Cliff is out. Laura finds her in agony.

Judy leads her into her bedroom, shuts the door, and removes her top and elasticated pants, exposing the red, raw pulp of her skin and the offending G-tube erupting out the middle of the mess and lying on some padding. Laura swallows. Judy lies down on her bed and directs her. Laura unhooks the leg bag from the G-tube, undoes all the tape holding it in place, removes the padding that both protects and secures it in place, grasps its end, and pulls. It slides out, blood and pus caking the exterior, Judy's body contracting down the hole. Laura throws the G-tube away and goes to pick up the new one.

"Leave it," Judy commands. Salt water trickles down her face. She just wants some respite from that thing inside her. Laura sits back as Judy breathes deeply and sinks into the luxury of baring her troubles. They talk for fifteen minutes, Laura every now and then wiping the drops of stomach acid that dribble out the hole and, when Judy grows silent, spilling her own problems into Judy's willing ears. Too soon, though, Judy knows that she must get back to her daily life.

Laura unwraps the Malecot catheter and looks at it. A line demarks how far to put it in. She starts pushing it into the fistula. Judy yelps. Laura pauses and then continues to feel her way through the track gently, trying not to push it into the fistula wall. She listens to Judy's breathing to know if she's on the right path. Finally, it's all the way in, but Judy whispers to her to pull it out a little bit. She can feel that it's too far into her stomach.

Judy lies on her bed, letting the waves of pain subside, continuing to direct as Laura tapes the G-tube in place, dabs cream on the angry skin, puts padding in place, hooks up the leg bag, and straps the bag to her leg.

Oh Lord, Laura prays, please, just once, I'd like to see this person healthy.

After ten minutes, Judy sits up, signalling she's ready to get on with her day.

For a few years, Laura helps Judy endure the torment of her G-tube. Sometimes, she has to go over in the evening, but Cliff stays seated in his chair, reading the paper studiously when she does.

Judy knits Laura a sweater in gratitude. She seems to know just when Laura needs her gift, as her friend has started to find the job taxing and is feeling unappreciated. When Judy hands her the sweater, Laura bursts into tears, embarrassed. Oh Lord, how could I have thought this? This woman is dealing with so much, and you're worrying about yourself, and here she's knit you a sweater.

In 1989, things explode. Blood joins the discharge out of her G-tube, and Jeej puts her on omeprazole (Losec) on December 13; use of this experimental drug requires Health Canada permission and mounds of paperwork. He hopes the new drug will counter the acidity of her discharge and heal the ulcers. She later goes on morphine suppositories and later still on morphine injections. Every night in the waning days of 1990, as he has been taught, Cliff swabs her arm, pinches her skin, and shoots the painkiller in.

The year 1990 has been long, Judy thinks as she stares out the window after unhooking herself from her TPN. From the high of the annual Oley Conference to the lows of her bones breaking, her G-tube deteriorating, and Jeej moving from TGH to St. Michael's Hospital despite the fight the HPENners waged with

TGH's administration, it's been a very long year, and it's not over yet. Sun dots the lake with sparkles, and a soft breeze flurries the water. Clouds puff across the September-blue sky. It's a bit cool for so early in the month. The glass cuts her off from the warmth of the sun; she cannot see the day's beauty for the pain and nausea. She turns away to make the bed and then goes into the bathroom. Suddenly, she's falling. She hits the electric radiator and ricochets into the towel rack. She's out cold on the ground.

The bathroom floor feels hard against her head. She opens her eyes and sees the ceiling. Nausea overwhelms her; she turns and lifts herself to the toilet and vomits—twice. She hates that. She sits up and feels the back of her head. A small spot there hurts as does her lower back. At least she did not pee in her pants.

She calls Cliff. She walks awkwardly to the car, and he helps her in. Susan waves good-bye as they drive past on the way to St. Mike's, Jeej's new place of business.

Jeej is much happier at this downtown-Toronto Catholic hospital, where the homeless regularly appear in the emergency ward. The staff members, from the orderlies to the nurses to the physicians, love their work, their patients, and their colleagues, and it shows. Jeej's administrative bosses crow about landing an internationally renowned physician and researcher. He's re-energized with the challenge of creating a nutritional program. There's only one problem: TGH fought him and St. Mike's tooth and nail for the millions of dollars in TPN-program funding. TGH won.

At the same time as she was cradling a broken elbow and painful ribs, Judy had led the battle to try to keep Jeej at TGH with the TPN-program funding. But she and her fellow HPENners lost. Now every time she's sick, like this morning, she must choose between seeing Jeej (the man who saved her, who knows her best, who's the most qualified to help her, but who works in a hospital where no one else understands TPN and the needs of TPN patients) or going to TGH (where the nurses know her and how best to care for TPN patients, but the system doesn't care). This morning, she chooses Jeej.

He ups the dosage of her drug, but the G-tube continues to leak and leak, and the drug changes her secretions. To make matters worse, some of her stomach contents have percolated over the years into the blind duodenal loop that Langer had created back in 1970. This percolation has stretched the blind duodenal loop into a sack in which the stomach juices ferment. On top of that, some of the stomach acid has eaten through the scars and tunnelled its way through the fibrous tissue in her abdomen, creating a fistula to her rectum—one more track for the juices to exit out of her. It reeks when she sits for long moments on the toilet. She hates it.

Cliff tries to cheer her up. He keeps the boat topped up with gas so that he can take her out on the water at a moment's notice while the weather is still warm enough. He sees she's unable to bend because of her raw side, and he takes over the dusting, the vacuuming, and the laundry. Even on her relatively good days when she insists on washing the clothes and hanging them out to dry, he carries the laundry basket outside for her. He tells her not to go making fancy meals for him, but she continues to buy regular chicken—cheaper than skinless, boneless chicken—and then to skin and debone it for him. She still worries about his health.

One morning, Judy sees "coffee grounds" secreting out the G-tube. It is coincidental to going on the Losec, but it makes Judy more nervous about taking the drug. The thick, brown secretions, flecked with black clots of blood, plug up her G-tube. Judy calls Marlene.

Marlene is still at TGH, but has continued to stay in touch with Jeej about Judy's increasing ordeal. Nevertheless, it's not the same as working side by side every day to help their star patient.

Marlene suggests irrigating her G-tube. Judy tries Coke. Then, in desperation, she tries having Cliff suck it out. When Judy confesses what she'd asked Cliff to do, Marlene is appalled and explains that the vacuum pulls her tiny stomach into the tube, ulcerating it in the process, making it worse. Judy stops it. She decides instead to decrease her Losec gradually, and for a time, her G-tube becomes less painful. Then the stomach acid starts corroding her skin again. A crater forms and grows. Her wounded flesh weeps.

One night, Judy cannot take it anymore. She holds firm against the pain until dinner is over, until Cliff leaves for his nightly run. Judy watches him through the window until she no longer sees his breath puffing in the December air. She dials Marlene's number. With each numeral she dials, her control slips a bit, and her despair rises until sobs pour out of her when she hears Marlene's non-threatening hello.

"What's wrong, Judy?" Marlene asks and waits patiently until Judy can talk, knowing it's the G-tube. Although they're also having trouble keeping her in metabolic balance—with so many electrolytes being washed out of her stomach—and in a good nutritional state, it's always the G-tube that Judy calls about.

"If this is what my life is going to be like, I don't want to go on any longer!" Judy cries.

Marlene respects Judy too much to say something as daft as "It will get better" or "You don't mean it—it's just the pain talking." Instead, she encourages her to talk.

"I can't live like this," Judy weeps convulsively as the changes she's endured flash through her mind: her cherished volunteering becoming a thing of the past, her mobility giving way to slings and crutches and a wheelchair, her bones breaking in her elbow and ribs, her fall, her infected hip. She's missed church, and her friends have brought the Bible study to her. "I've been through so much, I can't keep going." She's marched, endured, fought, survived, loved, and served for twenty years. She can see the end of her marathon. Even though she is still not a quitter, she is a realist. She knows death has her firmly in its grip. She who used to fall asleep as soon as her head would hit the pillow, she cannot sleep for the pain. She had even settled her legal affairs this past fall. She is exhausted. She is worn out. "I don't want to live like this," she whispers.

Judy stops, depleted from her venting. She grips the receiver, as Marlene starts speaking to her with her kind voice, her gentle compassion. Marlene's comfort calms her. Judy looks up and sees Cliff jogging out of the darkness toward the house. She says good-bye quickly, dries her face, and greets her husband with a smile.

He knows.

Soon after that day, Cliff arrives home from work and walks in on Judy screaming and screaming and screaming in the middle of the living room as blood and mucous and stomach acid stream out her G-tube, soaking the padding and splashing down her hip. Cliff drops his car keys and calls Marlene, panicked. Marlene calmly instructs him to double up on her Losec, hoping that will dry up her secretions. Cliff brings Judy her pills, tells her to swallow them, and soothes her. On December 19, he drives her to St. Mike's ER, but she manages to get released two days later. She just wants to get through one more Christmas at home with her family. She wants just one more chance to watch Cliff put the turkey in the oven according to the instructions she gives him from her chair, one more chance to savour the scent of the cake that Susan brings over for the family, one more chance to watch her grandkids open their presents, one more chance for her smiles to return. Then, she knows, she will have to go back in.

Chapter 28

Despair

As Judy gets through her one more Christmas, I'm hearing rumblings that she isn't doing well. Although I'd moved out of my parents' home more than three years earlier, I still see some of my dad's colleagues socially and have dinner most Sundays at my parents' place, where I get to hear what some of the TPN patients (those I've met through my research work or socially) are up to. I notice the worry in the air over Judy.

One Sunday—February 3, 1991, to be exact—my parents' white wall phone shrills its old-fashioned ring. "Can you get that?" Mum yells from somewhere. I run.

"Hello?" I answer breathlessly.

"Is Jeej there?"

I can hear the worry in the man's voice. "Yes, he is. I'll go get him." I shout, "Dad!" No answer. I put the phone down on the Formica kitchen table and shout again. Dad pokes his head out of his office. "It's for you!" I yell up the stairs at him.

"Who is it?" Dad asks.

"I don't know."

"Oh." He clunks down the stairs and picks up the phone. "Hello?"

"Jeej, it's Cliff."

"Oh, hello."

"Jeej, it's Judy. She's real bad." His voice cracks. "Jeej, she's going to die! She's going to be dead in an hour." Only minutes earlier as Cliff had walked into TGH for his weekly visit, he'd been thinking she's coming home. Instead, he finds her bloated, pale, and semi-conscious, imprisoned between the side rails of her bed.

"What?"

"You gotta do something."

"Calm down. What exactly is the problem?"

"Last week, she was healthy, Jeej. She was coming home. Now, she's gained seventy-five pounds in water in a week, Jeej! And they've done nothing. Nothing. They've just given her morphine for her pain."

"If she's only getting narcotics, I think that's inappropriate."

"You gotta do something."

"Well, if you want me to do something, you transfer her to me. I cannot believe that they've let her get that bad."

"They have!"

"Look, have the intern call me."

"Okay." Cliff rousts the nurse to get the resident to call Jeej, and then he phones Marlene. When she answers, his fear of losing Judy tumbles out of him in incoherent speech.

Marlene labours to understand him. She assures him that the decision to move Judy is theirs and that she supports it. But she reminds him that St. Mike's does not have staff other than Jeej versed in TPN patient care. "If he should leave to lecture outside of the country ..."

Cliff agrees, but asserts, "Judy will die this way." He hangs up to call their other TPN friends.

Marlene replaces the receiver and turns to her husband, Eric. She asks rhetorically how Judy could have deteriorated in only two days when she'd almost been ready to go home when Marlene saw her last. Months and months of caring for Judy from home, from TGH, from St. Mike's has worn Marlene down. She doesn't know what else to do.

Within the hour, an ambulance speeds Judy through the near-empty streets to St. Mike's, where she is wheeled straight to her room on 5B at 5:45 PM. Cliff and Judy wait for Jeej.

New voices penetrate the silence of the floor. Cliff turns his head expectantly toward the door as Jeej steps inside the room, resident and nurses in tow.

"Oh my God! What in hell have they done to you?" Horror at Judy's condition having forced the exclamation out of his mouth, Jeej regains his professional control and examines her. He sees a brighter-than-beet-red G-tube site, eroded fat, exposed muscle, and a glistening stomach through the maw. He sees a rash bubbling down her side, on her back, and over her buttocks. The rash is cellulitis. He smells rotting flesh. She has sepsis.

Jeej pulls Judy's gown back down and the sheet up over her. He steps back to face both her and Cliff and pauses to think. The little group of patient, husband, resident, and nurses watch Jeej, waiting for him to speak. "You have sepsis." Seeing the puzzled looks on Judy and Cliff's faces, he explains this condition rapidly and matter-of-factly. "Sepsis is a generalized infection. The measures I'm going to prescribe shortly are designed to bring the sepsis under control and eradicate the source of the infection. You see, the bacterial toxins in a septic person secrete cytokines, which dilate the blood vessels, change the permeability of the capillaries' walls so that they leak, and cause widespread damage to the major organs. This is a very serious inflammation. It can spread and become quite a serious problem. If sepsis isn't brought under control, it can lead to multisystem organ failure from these leaky capillaries. MSOF is a serious problem.

"Leaky capillaries in the kidneys reduce perfusion in the kidneys, which affects the electrolyte balance and urine output and leads to renal failure, kidney failure. You see? Leaky capillaries in the skin cause the fluid in the blood vessels to ooze into the spaces between the skin cells, swelling the skin, a condition called edema. When capillaries leak into the heart, they flood the heart muscle with fluid, congesting the heart and reducing the volume of blood the heart pumps in and out. This problem causes the heart to beat faster but with more effort because the muscle itself is congested, leading to cardiac, that is heart, failure. Capillaries also leak into the brain, reducing the volume of blood and the quantity of vital glucose to brain cells, as well as swelling the spaces between the cells, squeezing them together and leading to confusion and eventual unconsciousness. We want to avoid that. Leaky capillaries in the liver, which metabolizes nutrients, reduce the liver's protein production and skew its metabolism, causing hepatic or liver failure. Leaky capillaries in the stomach alter the stomach's lining in such a way that the acid is able to eat away at the stomach, and the stomach bleeds. You see? Lastly, leaky capillaries can drown the lungs; this is called pulmonary failure.

"Now, we don't understand this process of MSOF very well. But I'm going to try and prevent it from happening to you." What he neglects to add is that although doctors usually kill the infection, the catalyst of MSOF, the process the infection starts kills the victim 80 percent of the time. He continues, "I'm getting Dr. Soutter in to see you in case it requires some incision and draining. The concern I have is that I don't quite know how to heal it because there is a foreign body there, there is a tube there, and the tube will keep the inflammation going. And yet I can't take the tube out, because if I take it out, there is not a way by which your stomach could drain. You see? So this is a serious problem."

"What are you going to do to me?" Judy blasts him with questions. "How are you going to heal me? Am I going to get better? Are you going to do any painful things?" She fears most the NG tube: "Whatever you do, don't put that in."

"I can't promise you that."

"I don't know if I can tolerate the added pain of the procedures. How long am I going to be in hospital? When can I go home?"

She takes a breath, and Jeej answers as best he can, knowing that she's deeply worried that she's more sick than she should be and that she's not going to get better, knowing that normally she views her illness more as an opportunity for the staff to inflict discomfort upon her than as a gateway to death.

He flies into action. He has his residents Drs. Baxton and Lilly administer antibiotics to fight the cellulitis, and he has the dreaded NG tube put in because the G-tube cannot drain the secretions spilling out of her stomach fast enough. He telephones Soutter to discuss her G-tube, and he relays to Judy and Cliff the two options the doctors see. They can put a tube down her nose and suck her stomach contents out, then remove the G-tube and allow it to drain. Or they can insert a balloon in the fistula between the duodenum and the colon so that the gastric juices will flow out that way, obviating the need for the G-tube. The doctors prefer the second option because then they can take the foreign body out permanently. But Judy fears the risk and newness of the procedure. She goes with the first.

Jeej leaves to talk to Soutter, the surgeon, and Judy has a chat with the residents and nurses buzzing round her, informing them that she knows her disease, knows her pain, and knows when she needs pain meds and in what amount. They agree on Baxton setting the parameters and the nurses giving her morphine when she requests it.

At 9:00 PM, while Lilly starts a new normal solution for her TPN line and the nurses insert peripheral IV lines for the antibiotics and pepcid, Baxton fills her wound with duoderm granules. The tiny, hygroscopic, tapioca-like particles of this absorbent powder soak up the pussy secretions while protecting the wound, healing it from the bottom up instead of just superficially at the top. Every now and then, a resident or nurse scoops out the old granules and pours in fresh ones. With each change, the wound cleans up and the inflammation shrinks.

Monday dawns. Cliff leaves to pace in the hall when Soutter arrives with Baxton and sundry interns to examine and change her G-tube at 10:30 AM. He inserts a larger sump drain and sutures it to the flange. The sump drain works by pumping air into one tube and sucking the stomach contents out the other. Soutter's team places a slim barrier dressing around the G-tube; it decreases the secretions oozing out of her and collects them neatly in a bag. A nurse escorts Marlene into the room in the middle of this procedure. She and Soutter talk about what's been happening since the fall and whether a new drain she learned about at the just-finished ASPEN conference, one that drains both the stomach and the duodenal loop, will help. Marlene agrees to buy it from the Canadian distributor when she gets back to her TGH office. Everyone but Marlene leaves. She sits down beside Judy. And Judy weeps torrentially.

She's in so much pain. She's scared. She feels it's all so undignified. The system has let her down; she's falling through the cracks. How can this happen? Why did nobody do anything at TGH? Why can her G-tube not be fixed? Why does she have such a massive infection? What's going to happen to her? To her catheter? She rages about TGH's utter lack of care. Yet she's grateful that Jeej had her transferred and that finally someone is caring for her. Marlene coaxes Judy to tell her what had happened on Saturday and Sunday, but Judy's terror drowns her ability to hear and respond. She fears for the future of the TPN program and her fellow HPENners. Who is going to care for them with Jeej at St. Mike's and the funding restricted to TGH? Are they always going to fall between the cracks? She dreads her future. She gets angry. Her tears fall as fast as her gastric secretions stream out. The nurses, in and out through all of this, try to alleviate her pain. Cliff returns, and his distress mingles with Judy's as he repeats over and over to Marlene how he just had to do something. He'd done the only thing he knew to do to save Judy's life: he'd called Jeej.

Judy's sobs stop. Cliff's retelling of his part stops. It's quiet.

"I've resigned," Marlene tells them.

"We've lost Jeej. Now we are losing you. What are we going to do?" Judy wails.

"After this, Judy, it doesn't matter whether I have a job or not. I would have quit today." Today is Marlene's last straw. Judy had lain in one of Canada's top hospitals, deteriorating visibly over the weekend under the eyes of the staff. The resident's response was to pronounce this case difficult and to wait until Monday to consult with Jeej and the new head of the TPN program. The nurses had never called Marlene about Judy's deterioration or asked her to help. Judy's right; the system had failed, and not for the first time. Marlene is exhausted trying to anticipate where the system will fail next and to patch the leaks before they spread into puddles and floods.

Around noon, an orderly pushes in a wheelchair to take Judy for chest and abdominal X-rays. Marlene and Cliff leave. When the orderly pushes her back into her room, one of her TPN friends, Mary Bigelow, is waiting. The orderly parks her next to her bed and walks out. Judy asks Mary to help her back into bed.

Mary tries, but she cannot manoeuvre the dead weight of Judy's slumped body. Her mind boggles that this huge, helpless woman is Judy. She finds someone to help her and stays with Judy for awhile. To all the lifeliners, Judy is an independent, strong woman who fights illness with vigour and determination. But this woman cannot help herself; she's frightened and despondent and pleads with Mary not to leave. For four hours, Judy tells her tale and describes the mess they made of her at TGH. Judy wonders how much more she can endure; she questions if life is worth this level of suffering. Mary listens to this Judy, one she has never known before, and leaves only when Cliff returns.

With Cliff at her side, Jeej directing her care, friends visiting regularly and listening to her venting, the nurses caring for her actively, and the residents constantly checking on her progress and changing her medications or creams if they feel something else will heal her faster or better, she feels safer, taken care of, and loved. Her stress drops. Her emotions quieten. Slowly, slowly, she starts to mend.

Julie decides uncharacteristically to call her mother on Tuesday, instead of the usual Saturday. The person on the phone at TGH tells Julie that her mom has been transferred to St. Mike's, and Julie tracks her down.

Judy thrills to hear her daughter's whispery voice. She retells her tale and ends with an upbeat assurance that she's coming home in two weeks, but she cannot keep her despondency from seeping out. She cannot even answer Julie's question as to what to tell Miriam. She leaves it up to her.

Meanwhile, Miriam had called TGH on Sunday and, receiving no answer, had tried again on Monday. Then she had phoned her parents' place. There was no answer. Eventually, she calls Julie. Julie hesitates. Then she blurts out that she doesn't know if she's supposed to tell Miriam where Mom is, but she does.

No one telephones Cyndy. Judy, who always calls her eldest daughter whenever she's in hospital, does not this time. And Cliff, knowing it's cruel, just cannot deal with her and with Judy at the same time. He's too overwhelmed. He only wants Judy.

By Wednesday, Judy's emotional crisis is over, and by Thursday, she is feeling jaunty. She walks up and down the hallway twice, peeking into adjoining rooms and picking up all the hospital gossip. She talks to Miriam on the phone and blithely reassures her that she does not need to visit, knowing how busy she is helping her boyfriend to pack and move. She wants Miriam to be happy, not pressured by a complaining mother. Nevertheless, Miriam visits after dinner, to Judy's delight. Judy shares her tale with her daughter and, after having exhausted that topic, asks Miriam about the school she's teaching at, her boyfriend, her finances, her new house, and her feelings about all that. She asks her to bring wallpaper samples down for her to see and suggests she'll drop by when they release her. Her eyes don't leave her daughter's face, and her smile doesn't stop.

The hours fly by. Miriam says that she'll visit again and will bring her boyfriend. Judy basks in the afterglow of the visit and cogitates about how she'll keep Cliff from seeing the boyfriend. She, like Cliff, does not approve of him, but she isn't about to let anyone get in between her and Miriam.

She brings it up with Julie during their Saturday call. She worries about the friction between Cliff and Miriam and really hopes Miriam will visit weekly. Judy tells her about St. Mike's and then asks to speak to her grandchildren. Her voice soars and her laughter rumbles as she talks to each in turn about their latest antics.

Feeling that Judy is safe, Cliff heads home on Sunday after ensuring that Mary, Judy's "Sunday babysitter," arrives before he heads out into the bitter cold. The two women plan the upcoming trip to the 1991 Oley Conference and laugh themselves silly over old road-trip stories. They remember the time Judy got out of bed in the middle of the night to go to the bathroom and knocked the lamp over the bed, flipping the glass shade onto her head like a hat. Then they remember when the hotel fire alarm roused them from sleep and sent them running outside in their nightgowns with their IV poles.

After the laughter dies, Judy's worries crowd in again. She talks about Cliff's nerves and frets about how to end his depression. She wonders about how she can bridge the void between Cliff and Miriam and Cyndy. She hopes he is looking after himself properly and eating well. And she misses Bandit, her furry baby, a small dog. This Judy, Mary knows.

On Monday, restlessness takes over. Judy cries when she sees Miriam walk in with Jeej. She wants the NG tube out, and she wants out. They listen. They bolster her spirits and allay her fears. Jeej promises to look into taking out the NG tube. The next day, she gets her wish. After it slithers up her throat and down her nose and out, the relief at feeling nothing relaxes her immeasurably. Her strength returns. Her skin heals to a healthy pink. It's no longer tender; it's dry and intact. For the first time since 1970, Judy's G-tube site closes completely. For the first time in twenty years and four months, no acid bites into her skin.

Several months earlier, Jeej had agreed to speak at a conference in Belgium and another in Scotland. Since his wife, my mother, had not seen her sister Pat, who lives in Lincolnshire, England, in six years, they had decided to nip over after the Scottish conference. Mum worries about Aunty Pat's poor health. Because of the way England's health system is set up, Aunty Pat has no choice in which doctor she can see, even if he is completely incompetent. To make matters worse, English patients don't question their all-knowing physicians. The only time she's received good treatment was when her GP was on holidays and his temporary replacement looked after her. Mum plans on intervening. Aunty Pat's situation is much like Judy's: both are denied their choice of physician purely for economic and political reasons, not for medical ones. They discuss if he should still go, but Judy is doing so well and the staff is so attentive that he thinks it'll be okay. Also, Mum is anxious to see her sister.

As usual, Mum leaves their itinerary, hotels, and phone numbers with us, her children, in case of an emergency. The only problem in communication would occur when they are at Aunty Pat's because her phone prevents people from making outgoing calls. They would have to rely on people calling in to keep him informed.

Before he leaves on Friday, Jeej examines Judy one last time. She doesn't want him to leave. He assures her he'll be in telephone contact and that the residents will be able to track him down any time she needs him. She has faith only in him. She's nervous about other doctors running things. She doesn't know the St. Mike's staff as well as the TGH staff, and though she likes the people helping her, no one replaces Jeej. Plus she cannot leave the hospital until he returns—in two weeks. She reluctantly watches Jeej leave. She feels bereft.

Judy hears a noise at the door. It's Julie. In her angst, Judy unloads on Julie in a way she hasn't done before. She feels too weak for Jeej to leave; she wishes Cliff would stay more often, even though she knows he has to return to work; she doesn't understand why Miriam won't visit more; then she broods that Miriam and her boyfriend will show up while Cliff is with her. She's tried to arrange visits to avoid that because she doesn't want any tension. She doesn't know how she's made it this far. Before she came here, the pain had been eating away at her sanity. She'd thought she'd lose her mind. She'd thought she'd tear her hair out. She asks Julie to refill her glass.

As at TGH, Judy ruminates about the political situation at St. Mike's. The administration is shutting down certain wards and sections. While lying in bed, hearing the ambulances scream in and reports over the PA system, and listening to people trot up and down the hallways, Judy has questioned why anyone would cut back beds when they are needed desperately. The number of beds ought to match the number of people who need them, not satisfy some bean counter's numbers, she asserts. Julie never knows quite how Judy has acquired her intimate knowledge of the hospital's political and economic state when she is so ill. Julie stays with her all day, and Miriam joins them at 6:30 PM. Judy sees her two daughters together with her and doesn't want them to go, but she's tired, and the night is drawing to a close.

Julie returns Saturday for a brief visit before catching the bus home to Bobcaygeon. During this second visit, Judy focuses on Julie. "Is Gordon still working? How are the kids' report cards?"

Julie answers in few words, as is her nature.

Judy continues to talk as Julie puts on her coat and hat and mittens, asking her to convince Cliff to stay the next time he comes to Toronto.

Judy walks down the labyrinthine hall with Julie to the elevator. As Julie pushes the button, Judy repeats, "When you go home, phone your dad and try and talk him into staying down." Julie steps into the elevator. Judy says, "I love you and always will." The elevator doors shut.

She turns and walks slowly back to her room. She pauses at the nurses' station to chat a bit and remarks that she is thirsty. She continues into her room and climbs into bed. She pulls the bed tray closer to her and laboriously prints letters to her grandchildren and to Julie telling them of her undying love. Her writing, always so neat and perfect is now childlike, and it slips down off the small pages.

Chapter 29

The Battle Is Done

Judy is at her ideal weight, her G-tube is draining well, and healthy pink skin surrounds the site. It's Monday, February 18, 1991, and Judy is chatting up Lilly while he's examining her. His smile fades, though, when he realizes she's become intolerant to some of the nutrients in her TPN solutions. He leaves to work on her regimen.

At 3:30 PM, the nurse takes Judy's temperature—38.7 degrees Celsius. She pages Baxton, and he races over.

"How do you feel?" Baxton asks.

"No worse than usual," Judy replies glibly.

He's not so sure. Her abdomen is mildly tender, and her skin yellow. He draws blood for culturing through her line and prescribes antibiotics while he waits for the results.

Judy's temperature rises to 38.8 degrees Celsius. Baxton prescribes Gravol. The hell of aggressive treatment begins again.

Lilly telephones Jeej's house that night and leaves a message for someone to call him. When I hear about the message, I remember Cliff's frantic phone call of two weeks ago and start worrying about Judy. I call Lilly back and give him my dad's itinerary and telephone numbers in Belgium and Scotland. Lilly catches him in the middle of a talk, but wherever my dad is and no matter the time, he always takes a call about Judy.

By Tuesday, Judy's fever has settled in. She feels parched. The pain bounces back, and back on Demerol she goes. When the orderly fetches her for an abdominal ultrasound at 11:00 AM, the nurses have to arrange her in a stretcher because she can no longer sit up in a wheelchair.

The orderly wheels her into a darkened room at 11:47 AM. The technician smears her belly with electroconducting jelly and, after sitting down close beside her, pushes a large wand over her skin to search for her spleen, liver, aorta, kidneys, and fluid collections. She finds Judy's spleen easily. It's sixteen centimetres long.

The spleen manufactures our killer immune cells. The infection had alerted the spleen to increase production of these cells to hunt down and engorge the invading bacteria. As the bacteria proliferated, so did the killer immune cells, and the spleen grew with each increase in cell production. But despite the ferocious counterattack of the immune cells, the microbial assault continues to take its toll on Judy's energy and emotional stability.

After the orderly wheels Judy back into her room and the nurses transfer her to the bed, TPN all the while still infusing into her, Baxton walks in to find Judy dehydrated and in shock. He immediately injects a bolus of normal saline into her line to increase the volume of fluid in her blood vessels and thus increase her blood pressure. At the same time, he discontinues her omeprazole, believing that might have allowed the bugs to grow again. He considers rehydrating her through both her TPN and peripheral lines. At this point, the enterostomal therapist strides in to renew the dressing and pouch over the G-tube at 3:30 PM. An hour later, the nurses remove them and apply gauze over the site. Then they put the dressing and pouch back on. They increase her pain medications.

Miriam saunters in, unaware of Judy's reversal.

"Meem, I'm so sick. I'm so sick. I've never been this sick," Judy repeats over and over when she sees Miriam, her face creased, her voice wispy.

Shocked, Miriam flies out to the nurses' station and screams at them, "What is going on?"

She freaks early the next morning, too, when she sees her mother in her darkened room with a pounding headache and being given increasing doses of Demerol. She finds Baxton and asks him to explain his plan. The enterostomal therapist and Judy's ward nurses, he explains, are all working to keep her G-tube site freshly dressed and from irritating her skin. They're sponging her hot skin to cool her down. He's changing antibiotics to find the right combination to beat the infection. He's changing her TPN solutions to best nourish her. Miriam listens to all this and then sees the clock. She has to leave for work, but not before she declares that she's coming back that night with her friend, a male nurse. He'll tell her what Judy's deterioration means.

When Miriam is gone, Baxton looks again at Judy's chart and culture records. Yesterday, there was g negative; today, heavy proteus pseudomonas, heavy streptococci, and two other g negative bacteria flourish in her G-tube. He asks Judy how she is feeling. Judy whispers that she feels very, very sick. He apologizes as he turns the light on to examine her properly. She's less jaundiced, but her abdomen remains tender. The G-tube is draining well without the pouch. And though she is still dry, she is starting to become edematous.

Baxton goes off service at 5:30 PM; Lilly comes on duty and checks in on Judy. He flushes her lines with urokinase, which has just arrived from TGH, in order to unclot them and rid them of any bugs. He had experienced some problems in getting the urokinase from TGH and hadn't thought to ask Cliff, much to Cliff's displeasure, for he and Judy had been part of the TPN program since its inception, and he knows more about the urokinase and how to get it than the staff at St. Mike's. He could have arranged for Marlene to send it to them immediately. Instead, it took TGH two days to ship it to St. Mike's.

That night, Miriam and her friend find her mother erratic and delirious, all control lost. Two IV poles stand on either side of the bed. Tubes full of liquids and drugs snake into her arms, and an oxygen mask dangles off her face. Oblivious to her chains, Judy is trying to get out of bed. Miriam rushes to halt her and to put her mask back on. Judy fights. Miriam wins temporarily. Suddenly, Judy yanks off her oxygen mask and starts gasping, pleading, "Phone Marlene, phone Marlene. Marlene'll know what's really going on."

"Mom, you've got to keep the oxygen on!" She puts her mom's mask back on and grabs the phone to page Marlene.

The call beeps Marlene's pager while she is lying back in a dentist's chair and having her teeth examined. Apologizing to her dentist, she borrows his phone and dials the number on her pager.

"Mom would like to see you," Miriam says.

"What's happening?"

"She's not feeling very well. They gave her some oxygen, just when she needs it."

"I'm in Barrie." Marlene looks at her watch. It's four o'clock. "Ask Judy if she wants me to come tonight, and it will be dinner before I can make it. Or is tomorrow okay?"

Miriam asks her mom if tomorrow is okay for her. "Mom said tomorrow would be fine."

"Okay. Can I speak to Judy?"

"Well, Mom's quite tired and exhausted. She said she'd speak to you tomorrow. She just wants to see you."

"Fine." But it isn't fine. Marlene doesn't really understand what is going on because Judy hangs on to her usual demeanour of not wanting to admit that all hell is breaking loose and that she needs her now even if it's an inconvenience.

That kind of playing down is typical for only those patients with truly bad, chronic illnesses.

Miriam hangs up and turns to see Judy putting her legs over the side of her bed. Her body needs air and nourishment and instinctively nudges her to sit up. But she tries to stand up, too. Miriam fights her back down and replaces the oxygen mask. Judy wants none of this.

Meanwhile, Miriam's friend watches the battle between mother and daughter. When he has to leave, he tells Miriam softly, "I don't really want to upset you, but there's the smell of a dead body in this room."

"Well, maybe you might be right, but I think it's just the smell of all the drugs and the smell of all this, you know, gastric juices and bile and all that kind of stuff." She doesn't want to hear what he has to say, what she brought him to tell her: the truth. Even so, she's so desperate that she calls her dad.

"Mom's sick. You should come down right away."

"She was okay on Sunday."

"Yeah, but I really think you should come down now."

He drives down against rush hour traffic shortly after St. Mike's also contacts him. When he arrives, he and Miriam speak with the resident, who explains that not keeping her oxygen mask on makes Judy delirious and fidgety and makes her want to get up. Miriam writes down her Stouffville school number in case there are any problems.

The doctor stops Judy's TPN that evening for three hours because Judy cannot metabolize and use any of the nutrients. An hour and a half later, another resident examines Judy. At some point, somebody prescribes heparin in a paradoxical attempt to stop her internal bleeding.

Sepsis consumes the blood factors required to clot the blood. Sepsis also causes the liver to reduce its production of the protein that aids clotting. At the same time, sepsis changes the lining of the blood vessels. Normal lining prevents clots from forming on it; altered lining allows the bacteria to form microclots, which further injures the blood vessels. Heparin dissolves these clots and so prevents more bleeding.

Then another resident orders the heparin stopped for six hours. An hour and a half later, Lilly reassesses Judy and resumes her TPN. At 1:30 AM, Judy wakes up, gasping from the pain lancing through her body. The resident restarts the heparin and orders oxygen, which she continues to resist. And so Judy's care goes.

The morning of Thursday, February 21, 1991, Judy moans to Baxton that pain burns in her chest and that she cannot breathe. He fits his stethoscope into his ears and asks her to sit forward. He listens as she breathes in and out according to his instructions. He hears crackles in her lungs—muscles not used to doing all the work are being used to inhale. This is known as bronchial breathing.

Next, he examines her face, arms, hands, chest, abdomen, back, legs, and feet. Both of her feet are now swollen from edema, and greenish fluid flows out of her G-tube. He increases the percentage of oxygen to forty, and he orders a stat ECG. They find infiltration in the upper zone of her left lung and increased density in the left base of the lung. The left costophrenic angle is blunted. Anxiously, he compares that to the ECG done three days earlier. It has changed for the worse. He has the IV nurse draw blood to measure how quickly Judy's blood is clotting. Then he has her start a second IV in Judy's right forearm. They ask her the standard three questions to ascertain her level of consciousness: "What day is it? Where are you? What is your name?" Judy answers them. It's 10:00 AM.

The doctors telephone Miriam.

They perform a pulmonary angiogram. Lying in the bed, looking up into the lights overhead, oxygen mask on, Judy dreads the coming procedure. Unable to cope, unable to breathe, in pain beyond belief, she lashes out at the nurses blindly and battles them to keep the mask off. The team tries to calm her down and gives her narcotics to ease her pain. Once she stops thrashing, the doctors start the three-hour procedure.

They insert a catheter into the right vein that runs up the thigh to the pelvis and push the catheter up the vein until it enters the large vein just under her clavicle and thence down into the right side of her heart. (All blood returning from the rest of the body flows into the right side of the heart, and then the heart pumps it into the lungs, where it is oxygenated.) Once the catheter tip is in place in the heart, the doctors inject dye into the catheter. The dye shoots out of the tip of the catheter into her heart. Tremendous warmth floods Judy's body, and she becomes faint. The heart pumps blood and dye into her lungs, and the latter highlights the lung's network of veins and arteries. They photograph it. Her left lung has collapsed at the base. Segments of her right lower lobe and possibly her upper lobe contain clots.

Miriam follows Judy into her room as she is wheeled back in. The nurses check her right femoral site where the doctors had inserted the catheter. It is dry. The nurses leave Miriam alone with Judy, an unrecognizable Judy. Judy is angry. She wants out of bed. She battles Miriam to get out. She convulses and speaks insensibly about driving a school bus. Miriam just wants someone in there to help her calm her mom down. Miriam wants to leave, and she's angry at the nurses for abandoning her. But she can't leave her mother alone.

Judy hollers that she wants to go to the washroom. Miriam tries to support her, but Judy shakes, and her legs give way. She cannot walk. Miriam cannot fathom giving her mother a bedpan, and she pushes the intercom button and yells up at the speaker for the nurses to come and give Judy a bedpan. They won't. Panicked, Miriam telephones Marlene and then Cliff at Helen Jolly's (a long-time friend in East Toronto who lives next door to her sister Vivian Larkin where Cliff is staying) to come back down. While she waits, she pummels the nurses and residents with the question, "What are you going to do for her?" All that long day, they promise her that they are going to transfer her mom to the ACU, but no beds are available. "No beds, no beds" is all she hears. They all have to wait for someone to get better, or to die, to make space for Judy.

Marlene finally arrives at 6:00 PM. Judy recognizes her, but is quite confused. "Where's the pain, Judy?"

"It's everywhere. It's all over."

Marlene places Judy's mask back on her face. Judy yells at her and rips the mask off. Marlene puts it back on and reasons with her as to why she should keep her mask on. Judy seems to understand briefly, but then confusion clouds her face, and she tears at her mask, shouting, "Don't do that. I know I have to do it, but don't do that!" Marlene patiently explains, and the two battle back and forth. For Marlene, it's like returning to that nightmare ten years earlier when they'd nearly lost her. Still, she stays to support Miriam and Cliff as they wait and wait and wait for the transfer to ACU.

An orderly comes in. He wheels Judy out of her room. She's moaning, her head is rolling back and forth, her muscles are restless, and she looks like a bagpipe with all her lines. The three watch her disappear down the hall to the ACU.

Ten minutes later, the ACU nurses and residents examine, interview, poke, and prod Judy. Edema engulfs her whole body. Her skin is hot and dry and yellow. She's polka-dotted with bruises. The bacteria are eating her capillaries' walls, and the vessels bleed silently everywhere. All the moisture has been sucked out of her mouth, yet copious amounts of greenish, putrid fluid stain her G-tube dressing. They ask her the standard three questions to ascertain her level of consciousness: "What day is it? Where are you? What is your name?" Judy does not answer. It's 10:00 PM.

Cliff and Miriam fearfully enter her room together. ACU policy dictates a five-minute visit once per hour only. The sight is unlike anything they have seen before. The technology is wondrous: a dozen monitors line the wall behind Judy's bed, wires curl and flow across the floor, and two nurses watch her constantly, using handheld calculators to keep track of her progress. They feel lost in this ocean of hospital machinery surrounding Judy.

Cliff takes Judy's hand in his shaking one and murmurs, "Hey, Bones." And then he stands and looks at her, unable to comprehend her state. Miriam glances at her father and then back at her mother. Time is up. They leave for the night, Judy in the care of strangers in the room that echoes with the beeps and hum of the equipment keeping her alive and fighting the bacterial invasion.

While Judy tosses and moans and opens and closes her eyes, the night nurses and residents watching over her increase her oxygen to 100 percent, relocate one of her IVs when the skin above it reddens, clean her mouth, change her stained dressings, reposition her while they cleanse and treat her skin, give her morphine more and more frequently, struggle again and again to draw blood from her scarred and flat veins, bathe her and calm her, once again change her dressing, and replace her bedpan with a catheter—all this between midnight and five in the morning.

When Lilly looks in on her the morning of February 22, he decides that her central line must be pulled ASAP. It must be the source of her infection. The ID consultant and his staff also believe that her TPN line is septic with Proteus vulgaris and agree that her central line ought to be removed and that a bronchoscopy be done. But Cliff rejects their idea. Judy would be petrified if she wakes up to find her line gone; furthermore, he knows more about her line than they do. They argue. But he refuses to budge unless Jeej agrees.

Lilly reaches Jeej, who tells him that the catheter is very old and liable to break if removed. He advises against it. Lilly goes back to discuss it with the ID staff. They believe that her shock is worsening and that the only remedy is to remove the line. Lilly calls Jeej again.

"Whatever you do, don't take the catheter out," Jeej orders Lilly.

Lilly again speaks to the ID staff. They reiterate that they have no choice. To complicate matters, nephrology refuses to put Judy on dialysis unless the surgeons remove her central line—there's no point treating her if the source of her infection remains inside her body. Marlene disagrees, Miriam believes the doctors, and Cliff refuses without Jeej's consent. Lilly goes back to the phone.

"Would you be absolutely against it, because the shock is getting much worse?" he asks Jeej.

Jeej, thousands of kilometres away and unable to examine Judy himself, can see their point. "I personally don't like the idea, but, you know, if the shock is getting worse and this is the only way that you can save her life, then chances are this is the source of the infection."

Lilly pushes home his point.

Finally Jeej declares, "Pull the catheter out. But I don't think this is going to solve the problem." He admonishes Lilly, "Don't forget, there's another catheter that's been left inside." In other words, the other line could also be the source, and removing the functioning line would solve nothing.

The catheter breaks in half during the operation. They replace it with a Hickman line.

When Lilly calls him frantic with worry over this further complication, Jeej senses that they are in a barrel at the lip of Niagara Falls. He outlines the two options they have: somehow extract the residual line angiographically or surgically (an option he warns Lilly that is not immediately viable because of the age and fragility of the line) or position the tip of another central line near the end of the old one. In the meantime, Lilly infuses antibiotics at the site to sterilize the line.

Edema continues to expand Judy like rising dough. Using their arsenal of drugs and solutions, they cannot stop the seepage from her capillaries into the surrounding cellular spaces. Judy no longer opens her eyes on command, although her reflexes remain strong, and she moves her arms and legs on purpose. Her eyes open suddenly and just as suddenly shut. She is cold. The new nurse on shift lays a warming blanket over her and then conducts her standard beginning-of-shift routine: check Judy from head to toe, noting all her vital signs; examine her lines to ensure the solutions still drip into her veins; look at the monitoring equipment; ensure the alarms are set; and check that the emergency equipment is ready for action.

Cliff finds comfort staying with his old friend Vivian. She and her sister Helen live side by side, running in and out of each other's houses as if the buildings were one. They take care of Cliff together, doing his laundry, cooking for him as per Judy's instructions, and listening for as long as he needs to talk.

He takes his time getting ready in the morning. For one thing, he goes to bed late and, for another, the doctors conduct their rounds in the morning. It's better to arrive after they've seen Judy. He takes the TTC to the hospital since parking is so difficult to find and expensive downtown. He walks through the automatic glass doors of the hospital's Queen Street entrance after lunchtime and finds his way through the ancient halls to the waiting room. He sits down, dreading his five-minute visit with Judy. Sometimes, he needs several hours to get up the nerve to go in and see her. But he knows that Judy knows he is there in the waiting room and that he always arrives at the same time after the noon hour and always leaves at 9:30 PM. Finally, he goes in.

Cliff takes her icy hand in his and speaks comforting words softly to her for as long as he can control his shaking body. Sometimes, he rubs her legs, trying to erase her aches and pains. This swelling body cannot be his Judy. Seeing his wife getting sicker and sicker is so very hard, his only comfort his faith in the nurses and doctors at St. Mike's. When it becomes too ghastly for his senses, often before the five-minute limit is up, he rushes out of the room.

Miriam joins him in the small, white-painted waiting room. She sits on one of the two chairs across from the one couch, in front of the table strewn with a few stale magazines. A TV stands in one corner; its dreary, flickering screen hypnotizes the room's occupants when they have nothing to say. Strangers wait with them, waiting for their loved ones to pull through or die, knowing that without ACU care all of them would surely die. Cliff tells anyone—them or visitors from Fenelon Falls or family—about Judy and the horrors of her condition. When she can't stand it anymore, Miriam flees to the nearby Eaton Centre. A couple of times, she convinces Cliff to accompany her to Mr. Greenjeans for its too-large burgers and Buffalo chips in order to break the monotony of the waiting room and as a more satisfying alternative to the snack bar downstairs. Cliff never leaves for long, though. Miriam needs the time off.

Saturday night, they learn that Judy has MSOF. The doctor outlines her problems in a matter-of-fact voice: encephalopathy, respiratory failure, renal failure, sepsis, hepatic insufficiency. The medical terms terrify them, yet mean nothing. Despite her horrible prognosis, all of the doctors and nurses treat her aggressively, which includes inserting a painful arterial line to monitor her blood pressure directly. But if Judy's renal failure becomes full-blown, her prognosis will worsen. Still, Judy recognizes them, and this buoys their hopes.

Judy's temperature drops to 34.5 degrees Celsius at 1:30 AM on Sunday in spite of the warming blanket. The nurses humidify her through the ventilator, trying to warm her internally. Then Judy's oral airway starts to bleed into her mouth. The nurses try to suction the blood out, but Judy bites down on the device. Her mouth remains bloodstained despite repeated attempts at suctioning. The nurses continue to deal with crisis after crisis until the penultimate one at 10:08 AM.

Judy's heart stops.

Alarms scream.

Dr. Guslits runs into her room and starts CPR. He converts her heart rhythm to a normal one with good blood pressure three minutes later.

Judy's heart races.

Guslits thumps her chest and recommences CPR. Her heart rhythm returns to normal. The nurses immediately check her baseline neurological status. It is fine. But now she has fractured ribs, a common side effect of CPR and not surprising, given her brittle bones.

Guslits talks to Cliff when he arrives at St. Mike's about her heart attack. He hypothesizes that her attack was a result of a pulmonary embolism, a small clot that had torn away from the wall of a blood vessel, travelled through her veins with the returning blood, and entered her lungs where it lodged itself, blocking off the artery and squeezing out life-giving blood. The long-term ramifications worry him. It is time to discuss a DNR, a "do not resuscitate" order.

Guslits broaches the topic carefully. "Although the heart attack has not changed her condition, she probably needs life support," he explains.

"She wouldn't want life prolonged artificially if there's no hope for survival," Cliff acknowledges reluctantly and agrees to a DNR order.

"We'll of course continue all of Judy's medications, but in the event of a second heart attack, we won't resuscitate her. You understand?"

Cliff nods and sits down, head in hands.

He tells Miriam when she arrives at 2:00 PM. She cries, "No, no, no! We want them to try everything!"

"If she's going to die, we should let her die on her own. When the time comes, it comes."

"No! I want them to try!" Her mom always fought for life; she will never give up fighting if she has a chance. The DNR is taking that chance away. Besides, she still has so much to say and to do with her mother that she is not ready to let go.

Miriam and Cliff argue until he agrees to rescind the order. They go to inform Lilly that she wants them to try CPR, but if unsuccessful after the first few minutes, the doctors should stop it. They agree to an autopsy since Judy will prefer that over having her body sent to a medical school. The ACU removes the DNR order officially at 8:00 PM.

Marlene spends that week with them, and when she's simply too exhausted to make the long trip downtown, she calls Cliff at Helen's at 10:30 PM, knowing he'll be there and still be wide awake talking to his friends about his day.

She sits between Cliff and Miriam. Cliff asks her about Judy's medical care, seeking to understand what his eyes cannot believe. Then Miriam asks her a question or asserts that Cliff just doesn't understand. Marlene turns back to Cliff and asks him what he thinks Miriam has to say. Slowly over the days, she translates less and less as they start conversing more and more directly to each other. Relieved at their detente, she asks Cliff where Julie is. He refuses to discuss it. He had in fact spoken to Julie. She had wanted to come down to support him, but Cliff told her that Judy is in a coma and would not want Julie to see her that way. And so Julie first keeps up to date through Miriam, then later through Cliff. But when she receives Judy's letters on Tuesday, she knows that Judy no longer wants to fight. Her death is coming. That same day, Cliff knows it too, as does Marlene. Neither can bear the thought of Judy being impaired or physically dysfunctional, assuming she survives her ordeal, and agree she is better off dying. They keep vigil.

Marlene and Cliff walk arm in arm into Judy's humming room with its LED readouts and steady beeping and hissing respirator. Although her clinical mind understands the Judy she sees, Marlene does not recognize her patient, her friend. Each time they visit, Judy is bigger. Her cheeks blow up, obliterating her nose; her eyes peep out from between her massive forehead and round cheeks; her lips swell; her arms grow to the size of a man's legs; her skin splits here and there; and her body spills over the confines of the bed.

They return to the waiting room with relief. Cliff talks for hours about Judy, their life together before 1970, and her strength. He weeps. Worry wrinkles his eyes and reddens their sockets. Suddenly, anger takes over, anger that her life cannot be in vain, that others should not receive the travesty of care she received at TGH. He vents his frustration with Miriam and asks Marlene to please reason with her about the DNR order.

She does so in private, listening with compassion to what Miriam thinks her mother wants, intuitively understanding Miriam is not ready to let go, educating her about the ramifications of the order, giving her the time she needs to mull it over, make peace, and assent. Miriam does so at 5:20 PM on Saturday, March 2, 1991. By this time, Judy has no neck, no chin, and no discernible features. Her eyes bulge out so much that the nurses had taped them closed for the duration of the visits. She lies motionless, looking like a great big balloon ready to burst. She weighs about one hundred and forty kilograms in water. No matter how much fluid is pumped into her blood vessels, more oozes out and into her tissues, leaving less and less blood for her heart to pump and causing her body to expand. The ACU staff had eradicated the infection, but lost control of the resultant metabolic effects.

Jeej flies back to Toronto late Friday night. On Saturday, he drives down to St. Mike's to see Cliff and Judy. Miriam looks up when she hears him walk into the waiting room. Her heart lifts—God has arrived. He will cure Judy, because Jeej can fix anything. He listens to their story and then goes in with Cliff to visit Judy.

When he last saw her, Judy was healthy and jibing him. Now, she is a large shell for her brave but tired spirit.

"What should we do?" pleads Cliff.

"The outcome is very poor, and, frankly, just continuing life support is not a very good idea. And that is the decision to be made," explains Jeej.

Cliff looks down at Judy. "You know, I think she's suffering too much, and she's going nowhere."

"Well, we could try one other thing. We could try to get some antibodies against endotoxins."

"Well, if that's what you think you'd like to do, try it."

But they do not.

Marlene telephones Cliff at Helen's that night.

Helen answers. "Hello?"

"It's Marlene Close, the nurse, calling."

Cliff takes the phone and with a quivering voice answers, "Hello?"

"It's Marlene. I just called to see how Judy was."

"Oh! You scared me half to death. Thank God. I thought for sure you were going to tell me she's dead."

"No."

"She's not going to make it, you know."

"I know."

"We renewed her DNR order and have stopped treating her aggressively. It's just a matter of time. I've made the funeral arrangements with her minister."

They say good-bye.

Miriam has come to terms with Judy's impending death. Julie knows. Judy spared Cyndy seeing her die. Jeej has flown home. Cliff has accepted.

Judy sinks into her ultimate crisis.

Her heart stops at 3:55 AM on Sunday, March 3, 1991.

Chapter 30

Resurrection

Judy looks dreadful to Laura's trained eye. She's huge. Substances pour out of her everywhere. Laura hops from one spot to another, mopping up the spillage with fresh dressings. As she dries one part of Judy's body, a leak springs forth from another, and she rushes to wipe it up. She runs out of dressings and leaves to fetch new ones. She hurries back into the room, but the bed is empty.

"Oh, my gracious, where is she? What's happened?" Questions tumble out of her and echo in the empty room as she looks frantically this way and that in vain.

"Laura."

Laura stops. She cranes her head up. Looking down at her from the loft over part of the room is Judy. She's sitting on the loft's edge, her smile filling the room with light. She's radiant. She wears no glasses. No tubes come out of her. Her skin shines. Her eyes sparkle. Her hair bounces with vitality, and it gleams in the light.

She is absolutely healthy. Laura cannot speak.

"I'm fine."

Laura wakes up with a smile. The pre-dawn hours of early-March darkness blanket the room. But she sees only the glow of Judy's perfect healing.

Epilogue

At the time of Judy's death, which the autopsy found was most probably due to septicemia, she was the longest-living person on TPN, surviving for about twenty years and five months. After her death, Doris Johnston took over that title. She went on TPN in October 1972 and was the third person to do so. Like Judy, she had been healthy most of her life, was married, and just wanted to go home and look after her five children. Unlike Judy, she eventually was able to eat and drink a little, although like most on TPN, she had to time her eating and drinking so that she wouldn't suddenly have to go to the bathroom in the middle of a midway ride. When most people on TPN have to go, they have to go now—no waiting. The only other person I have heard of who was like Judy, in that she could not eat one bite of food ever, was Sandra Lapenny. Doris died September 25, 2006 after being widowed for well over a decade, seeing at least nine grandchildren born, and remarrying. She lived on TPN for almost thirty-four years.

Today, TPN is used to help anyone who cannot eat or whose bowels do not allow him or her to be nourished from food (the latter may be able to eat but remain malnourished). This includes people with bowel diseases, cancer, AIDS, and cystic fibrosis, to name a few. It's used more often in the United States than in Canada, and physicians around the world have come to Toronto to study this technique or have learnt from Jeej at conferences in many, many countries. Jeej and Judy revolutionized nutritional medicine, and people everywhere continue to benefit.

Notes

All interviews were conducted by me, were on the record, and were taped with a couple of minor exceptions or the odd time when the tape cut out. Interviews were conducted between March 1991 and March 2000. I confirmed or corroborated information given to me by one interviewee with one or more other interviewees if possible and/or with written materials such as medical records, newspaper and journal articles, Judy's personal memorabilia, correspondence, Cathy Kelly's diary records, videotapes from Trinity United Church and Toronto General Hospital's fundraising campaign, and so on. The medical records included those from Judy Taylor's family physicians, Scarborough General Hospital (SGH), Toronto General Hospital (TGH), and St. Michael's Hospital. The articles are listed in the bibliography. Photographs from Dieter Baun, Dr. Langer, Carol McGregor, Dr. Patel, and Cliff Taylor were helpful in envisioning Judy Taylor at different ages and stages and some of the medical or surgical procedures. Newspaper articles often included photographs, and these were helpful too, including a clipping of one article by Susan Krajewski, complete with photographs of Judy with Cliff and Aunt Connie entitled "Mom Hasn't Eaten for 12 Years."

Chapters 1 to 13: I drew from interviews with Susan Madden, Marjorie Ste. Marie, Katharine Prouse, Sandra Lapenny, Fran Bartlett, Eileen Chapelle, Meryl Williams, Helen Jolly, Vivian Larkin, Harlan Kelly, Barbara Crowther, and the Taylors for the personal details of Judy's life growing up and life in Scarborough before and during Judy's time in hospital. Drs. Isaac, Jeejeebhoy, Johnston, Langer, O'Dwyer, Wright, and Zohrab, as well as Pat (Walker) Cascione and Dianne Garde, supplied medical details, explanations, and context of Judy's time at SGH and TGH. The medical records from Isaac and the two hospitals, although not as complete as today's records, described the minutiae of Judy's treatments and difficulties from the years before she became ill and was rushed to the ER at SGH to the day of her discharge from TGH in 1971. I read Judy's education records at Baron Renfrew, her elementary school in North York, and at Jarvis Collegiate Institute, one of two high schools she attended. The records at North Toronto Collegiate Institute had been burned in a fire a few decades back and thus were not available, and I was unable to see her records at Bishop Strachan School. Her personal memorabilia gave me a brief outline of her educational and music-education history from the time she was a child until she became a literacy tutor in 1987. Gloria Snyder, Cascione, and Jan Hague, along with Cathy Kelly's diaries, gave me insight into her non-medical life on the ward at TGH during those first ten months. I copied the letters Judy wrote verbatim, as I did elsewhere throughout *Lifeliner*. She'd started to write her biography, and those few pages confirmed some information. Details of the hospital environment came from my own memory or from Cascione.

Chapters 14 to 17: Much of the details of life with Judy—dinnertime, the supply runs, her essential fatty acid deficiency, and the barbecue—came from her children, Cyndy, Julie, and Miriam, and especially from her husband, Cliff Taylor. The medical information came primarily from Jeejeebhoy and the final summary that Zohrab wrote up for Judy to take home when she was discharged. I read the relevant journal articles as well. Many of my memories came into play when writing Chapter 17. George Tsallas talked to me about his time with Cliff during the supply runs. The conversation Judy had with a new TPN patient came from my interviews with her fellow lifeliners.

Chapter 18: The background information and details of Judy's life came from her family, Rev. Ed Bentley, Ann Beck, Ruth Belbeck, the Fletts, Doris Johnston, Joyce Junkin, Joyce Kimble, and her dentist, Dennis Richardson. The letters came from Judy's personal memorabilia and were copied verbatim, minus her address.

Chapters 19 to 20: The medical story of Judy's chromium deficiency was told to me by Jeejeebhoy, Tsallas, and Dr. John Da Costa. Bill Trent's article in *Weekend Magazine* in *The Globe and Mail* supplied some of the details of her symptoms, as did Cliff and Cyndy. Wretlind wrote to me about visiting Judy. Newspaper and journal articles were also helpful.

Chapters 21 to 22: Although some of Judy's friends and neighbours supplied a bit of information on her family difficulties, her family and Rev. Bentley were the main sources.

Chapter 23: I drew mostly from interviews with Cliff, Marlene Close, and Jeejeebhoy and from the medical records for this chapter.

Chapter 24: Prof. Arvid Wretlind, Britt Lindqvist, Ingalill Bergqvist, Dr. Erik Vinnars, Tsallas, Jeejeebhoy, and Close provided me with the bulk of the information for this chapter. Judy had saved the typed-up itinerary given to her, with her handwritten notes on it, and that provided the timeline as well as the dinner details.

Chapter 25: Medical records from TGH and Da Costa's office were very helpful, as were the relevant journal articles. Kimble revealed to me how Judy really felt about her hair. And, as always, I relied on my interviews with Jeejeebhoy and Cliff.

Chapter 26: Roslyn Dahl helped me get the facts straight as to the dates and names. Don Young, Dr. Lyn Howard, Lenore Heaphey, Close, Sandra Lacey, and Lapenny all gave me a good sense of this event and the importance of the Oley Foundation conferences to Judy. Judy's letters are copied verbatim, complete with spelling mistakes and minus her address. I copied her speech verbatim, but cleaned up the spelling and made some minor changes to reflect how her audience would've heard it. Cliff and Susan Clayton spoke to me about Judy's sense of the time she had left and her attitude toward life.

Chapters 27 to 29: These were difficult chapters to write. Almost everyone felt emotional about Judy's last days, yet they spoke to me at length about it. Cliff, Julie, and Miriam gave me the family's perspective. Jeejeebhoy, Close, and Garde provided the bulk of the medical perspective. I relied on the medical records from TGH and St. Michael's Hospital, as well as those from her family physician's office and the autopsy report. Lapenny and Mary Bigelow, as well as many others, gave me the friends' perspectives.

Chapter 30: This came straight out of my interview with Laura Armstrong.

List of Interviewees

Many people gave freely of their time in answering my questions about Judy Taylor, her life, and her total parenteral nutrition (TPN). The problem I had wasn't in finding people to interview about Judy but in deciding when to stop. Everyone wanted to talk to me about Judy. They loved her and respected her, and they wanted to share her with the world. They made it possible for me to write this book, and I am totally in their debt for their help and encouragement. In alphabetical order, here is the list of interviewees. I apologize for any errors or omissions.

Johane Allard, MD, FRCP (C): A gastroenterologist, she originally came to Toronto from Montréal with her family to study under Dr. Khursheed Jeejeebhoy as a fellow. She stayed on at the University of Toronto and Toronto General Hospital (TGH). The latter hospital asked her to take over Jeejeebhoy's position when he left for St. Michael's Hospital.

Lalla Armstrong: Sister of Laura, their mother was a church elder with Judy. She heard much about Judy before meeting her through the church choir in the mid-1970s.

Laura Armstrong: A nurse, she first met Judy when Judy drove down with friends to help move Laura back to Ontario from Newfoundland in 1981. She became essential to Judy in managing her G-tube in her last years.

Jo (Whitwell) Ayers: At the time that Judy's story unfolded, Jo went by the name of Jo Whitwell. She always brought laughter with her when she came to my parents' parties, and I didn't realize until I interviewed her how much she was involved in Judy's management of her G-tube.

Fran Bartlett: Fran was a neighbour of Judy's in Scarborough. She told me of the day that Judy went into hospital. And she told me about Judy's life in Scarborough before she went on TPN and moved up north to Bobcaygeon. Like Chapelle, Williams, and Dow, she gave me a sense of the kind of person Judy was before she became ill.

Dieter Baun, MS: Dieter was the pharmacist at TGH when my father developed TPN for Judy. He kindly leant me his slides, and he helped me understand the background of the formulae.

Ann Beck: A fellow churchgoer at Trinity United Church in Bobcaygeon, Ann met Judy through the choir and told me stories of Judy at the church socials and other Bobcaygeon events.

Ruth Belbeck: She knew Judy through Trinity United Church and, with Joan Handson, would drop in on Judy once a week to watch TV, sample muffins, and talk. Ruth respected her thoughts on life and felt she could tell Judy anything. She always sat across from Judy during weekly Bible study.

Florence Bell: A fellow lifeliner, she met Judy in the 1980s.

Rev. Ed Bentley: Judy knew several ministers, but Rev. Bentley was the one she confided in the most. It was through him that I came to see her beyond the mask she put on for everybody and to understand the family dynamics better. Paradoxically, what he told me about Judy and her anger helped me a great deal after my brain injury.

Ingalill Bergqvist: Ingalill was International Product Manager for Intralipid at KabiVitrum AB when Judy visited Sweden. She was instrumental in bringing Judy to Sweden as a speaker at the World Congress of Gastroenterology held in Stockholm in 1982.

Mary Bigelow: Mary was a fellow patient of my father's. She knew Judy well and helped me to understand not only the patient experience but also the relationship between Judy and her fellow lifeliners.

Joan Bishop: Currently Executive Director at the Oley Foundation, she was helpful in finding information on Judy at the Oley Conferences and photos of her.

Patricia A. Brown, RN, MSN, CNSN, OCN: Pat was an adviser to the Oley Foundation when she met Judy and is the Nurse Clinician, Clinical Nutrition at Memorial Sloan-Kettering Cancer Center in New York.

Rev. John Bushby: He was one of the ministers at the church Judy attended in Bobcaygeon.

Pat (Walker) Cascione, RN, DNA, BAS, CHE: Pat worked with Jeejeebhoy on using alimentation for the short-term on post-surgical patients before Judy arrived on her floor. She was Judy's chief nurse during her first stay at TGH from 1970 to 1971. She left the hospital in 1973.

Eileen Chapelle and Meryl Williams: They were Judy's neighbours in Scarborough, and Eileen worked for Dr. G. H. Isaac. Like the Taylors, they were original to the street. All their children played outside on the dead-end, court-like street.

Susan Clayton: Susan was a neighbour of Judy's in Bobcaygeon. What I remember most vividly from talking with her was her description of how Judy got people to put their own problems in perspective.

Marlene Close, RN, BScN, MScN: Marlene is a good friend of our family, and she was a key figure in Jeejeebhoy's team at TGH, starting as a young nurse. She was the youngest person appointed to nurse manager before becoming the Clinical Co-ordinator, Parenteral and Enteral Nutrition Program. It was in the latter capacity that she accompanied Judy to Sweden. After attaining her degrees, she became Clinical Nurse Specialist (CNS), Nutritional Support Program. Judy and Cliff came to lean on her more and more as Judy started her downward slide.

Barbara Crowther: Daughter of Harlan and Cathy Kelly, she sat in on my interview with her father and shared stories from a younger perspective and as the Taylor's babysitter.

John Da Costa, MD: Judy had three family physicians, or general practitioners (GPs) in Bobcaygeon, and Dr. Da Costa was the one she had the longest and who knew her problems best from a GP's perspective.

Roslyn Dahl: Currently Director of Communications and Development at the Oley Foundation, Roslyn supplied me with contacts and information about Judy and the award Judy received from Oley and the Oley Conferences.

Doris Dow: Doris knew Judy when Judy still lived in Scarborough. They met through Explorers at their local church, and Doris persuaded Judy to join her and eight other women for weekly bowling at the Parkway Plaza.

Mary Ellen and Ron Flett: Mary Ellen worked at the medical centre where Judy saw her last two GPs, including Dr. Da Costa. She took care of Judy by taking blood from her worn-out veins using butterfly needles or arranging tests whenever she walked into the centre for help. Mary Ellen had heard of Jeejeebhoy before moving from Toronto to Bobcaygeon with her husband Ron in 1985. The two also met Judy through the choir at Trinity United Church.

Don Freeman: Don first went on TPN at the Ottawa Civic Hospital under Dr. Dilip Patel, who used TGH's TPN training manual as a guide, as the Civic had not had a patient on TPN permanently before. Don founded the national association known as CPENA (Canadian Parenteral and Enteral Nutrition Association) in 1984. He travelled to meet with the Toronto group to talk about his association, and that's when he heard about and met with Judy.

Dianne Garde: Dianne trained as an enterostomal therapist at the Cleveland Clinic in 1969. She became the first such therapist in Toronto at TGH and first saw Judy shortly after she was transferred from Scarborough General Hospital in 1970. She last saw Judy at TGH in the weeks before Judy transferred to St. Michael's Hospital in 1991.

Marian Graham: Marian was Judy and Cliff's neighbour on Sturgeon Lake near Bobcaygeon. This was after they changed their minds about living in the town proper and decided to move back to the lake.

Jan Hague: Jan was admitted to TGH under Jeejeebhoy for tests. Being on the same ward in 1970 and 1971, Judy and Jan bumped into each other and became buddies.

Joan Handson: Joan attended Trinity United Church and noticed Judy singing up front in the choir. Gradually, the two became friends.

Lenore Heaphey: As Executive Director of the Oley Foundation in New York state, she first heard about Judy through Don Young. She finally met Judy at the Oley Foundation picnic and was totally amazed at how good she looked and how healthy and matter-of-fact she was. She used to telephone Judy to learn about the early days of TPN.

Nancy Hill: Nancy first met Judy through Trinity United Church when Nancy became a Christian in the late 1970s. She owned a craft shop, which Judy frequented, and went on a memorable road trip with Judy and Lalla Armstrong to move Laura Armstrong from Newfoundland back to Ontario.

Ted Hill: Ted was Judy's lawyer and Nancy's brother.

Lyn Howard, MB, BS: Dr. Howard modelled her TPN program on Jeejeebhoy's. She and a surgeon went up to TGH—as it was not that far from the Albany Medical Center where she was based in Albany, New York—to see how it was done. She didn't meet Judy then, but she had read much about Judy in the journal articles that Jeejeebhoy had written. She also heard about Judy through Don and first met her at an Oley conference.

Geoffrey H. Isaac, MD: Dr. Isaac was the Taylors' GP in Scarborough before they moved up north. He still saw them on occasion after that.

Khursheed N. Jeejeebhoy, MB, BS, FRCP (C): This is my father and the gastroenterologist who saved Judy's life. He received an MB, BS (medical degree) at Christian Medical College in Vellore (Madras, India) in 1959; an MRCP (Lond.) in 1961; a PhD from London University (thesis: "Albumin metabolism in gastrointestinal disease," which was recommended for publication in abridged form) in 1963; an FRCP (Edin.) in 1966; an FRCP (Canada) in 1968; and an FRCP (Lond.) in 1976.

He trained in Vellore and Ludhiana in India and West Middlesex Hospital in London, England. He has been registered with the College of Physicians and Surgeons in Ontario since January 4, 1968, the date he arrived in Toronto. He was a professor of medicine, cross-appointed as professor of nutrition and of physiology at the University of Toronto. He is currently an emeritus professor of medicine at the University of Toronto and Director of Nutrition Support at St. Michael's Hospital.

He belongs to the American Association of Physicians, American Society for Clinical Investigation, American Society for Clinical Nutrition, American Institute of Nutrition, American Gastroenterological Association, Canadian Association of Gastroenterology, Canadian Society for Clinical Investigation, Nutrition Society of Canada, and Ontario and Canadian Medical Associations. His awards include: Borden Award 1975; Canadian Association of Manufacturers of Medical Devices Award 1980; McCollum Award 1982; Sir David Cuthbertson Lectureship of the European Society for Parenteral and Enteral Nutrition 1982; Sir Arthur Hurst Lectureship of the British Society of Gastroenterology 1983; India Medical Association Recognition Award 1983; International Honourable Member of the French Society of Gastroenterology 1986; Crampton Award for Distinguished Service in Nutrition 1987; Varis Award 1988; Astra Foundation Lecture given to the Caledonian Society of Gastroenterology 1991; American College of Nutrition Award 1993; Dales Award of the University of Toronto 1993; Teaching Award, St. Michael's Hospital, 1994; Finkelstein Prize 1995;

Research Award from the Canadian Association of Gastroenterology 1996; Department of Medicine Research Award at University of Toronto 1997; Distinguished Service Award from the Canadian Association of Gastroenterology 1998; Distinguished Service Award from the Ontario Association of Gastroenterology 2000; C. Richard Fleming Lecture, Mayo Foundation 2002; Dr. Arthur Squires Teaching Award 2003 and 2004.

He has published more than one hundred books and chapters, including in *Harrison's*, and more than three hundred and fifty articles and abstracts in peer-reviewed journals. The medical residents, research fellows, and PhD candidates he taught and supervised practise all over the world.

Doris Johnston: Doris was the third person to go on long-term TPN. After Judy died, Doris became the longest-living person on TPN. (She is now deceased.)

K. Wayne Johnston, MD, FRCS (C), FACS: He was a surgical resident under Dr. Bernard Langer when Judy first arrived at TGH and assisted during her surgeries.

Joyce Junkin: A member of Trinity United Church, she organized the library and became the church librarian. She loaned me some videotapes that Judy appeared on. These were of church functions, indoor and outdoor. (She is now deceased.)

Meryl Junkin: Meryl first met Judy through the ACW group at Providence Church near Bobcaygeon. This was the church Judy attended when they went to their cottage during the summers before she became ill and went on TPN. She remained active in the group, as it's affiliated with the whole of the United Church, not just one particular church congregation, after going on TPN.

Shirley J. Junkin, MD: She was Judy's first GP in Bobcaygeon.

Harlan Kelly: He and his wife were the Taylors' neighbours up near Sturgeon Lake and knew them long before Judy became ill. Cliff had bought the cottage lot from the Kellys. His wife Cathy's diaries helped me understand some of the chronology of events and Judy's pre-TPN life.

Gail Kennedy, RN: She was a TPN teacher at TGH, starting in 1978. She and Jeejeebhoy's team used Judy as a morale booster and reassurance person with those patients who were having difficulty adapting to TPN.

Kathleen Killen: While in McMaster Medical Centre, Kathleen read articles on Judy when it looked like she would have to go on TPN permanently. Like so many, she heard about Judy from staff at TGH when admitted there as a patient long before she met her at one of the TPN clinics.

Joyce Kimble: She owns the hairdressing salon in Bobcaygeon that Judy frequented. Judy had much trouble with her hair after going on TPN, and Joyce tried to make it look nice for her.

Sandra Lacey: Sandra went on TPN in 1982 and, like so many, received a brief visit from Judy to reassure her about going on TPN. Sandra later became active in CPENA.

Bernard (Bernie) Langer, MD, FRCS (C), FACS: Dr. Langer was Judy's key surgeon and the one who invented her central line, or lifeline, through which the TPN solution flowed.

Sandra Lapenny: A friend and fellow lifeliner of Judy's who first met Judy at camp and then later in the hospital, she was president of CPENA at the time I started researching this book. She aided me a great deal, financially and otherwise, in my research and in understanding the TPN aspect of Judy's life. (She is now deceased.)

Helen Jolly and Vivian Larkin: Sisters and old friends of Cliff's, they first met him in 1953. Vivian opened her home to Cliff whenever Judy was in hospital and he needed a place to stay and park his car. The sisters gave me a clear picture of his life all the way back to before he met Judy and up until she died.

Britt Lindqvist: Secretary to the marketing director Rune Bergman at KabiVitrum AB in Stockholm, Sweden, she was Judy's escort to all the social functions during the World Congress of Gastroenterology in 1982. The two got to know each other quite well and kept in touch after Judy flew back to Canada. Britt arranged for Isaac Austin, an expat American in Stockholm who did much translation work for KabiVitrum, to translate the Swedish-language articles on Judy for me.

Susan Madden: Susan was a spry ninety-something lady when I interviewed her. First cousin to Judy's adoptive mother, she gave me much background material on Judy's family.

K. J. MacRitchie, MB: A psychiatrist, he wrote a paper in 1978 for the *Canadian Psychiatric Association Journal* entitled "Life without eating or drinking. Total Parenteral Nutrition Outside Hospital." He interviewed nine of the TPN patients for his research study and discussed their stages of adaptation in his article and with me.

Carol McGregor: Carol is Cliff's sister. She's younger than him by five years.

Michael G. O'Dwyer, MD: Judy's surgeon at Scarborough General Hospital

Dilip G. Patel, MD, FRCP (C): He started a one-year research fellowship with Jeejeebhoy in July 1971 and was involved with some of the metabolic studies done on Judy. He presented a paper on these studies to a visiting professor and afterward had Judy come down to meet the visitor; she looked not at all like a patient but like a healthy woman. Dr. Patel joined the gastroenterology department at Ottawa Civic Hospital to establish a TPN program there after the completion of his fellowship.

Katharine Prouse: Older cousin to Judy

Dennis Richardson: Judy's dentist in Bobcaygeon (He is now deceased.)

Olivia Saqui, RN: Olivia started working at TGH and with home-TPN patients in 1981, shortly after graduating with her RN degree from college. By the 1980s, Judy was so used to being asked by the new person on staff about her story that she just told it freely. Olivia became one of the team that Judy trusted so much with her life.

Gloria Snyder: She was a fellow patient of Judy's at TGH in 1971. As Judy became well, the two women socialized and together played pranks on the residents while in the hospital. They stayed good friends.

Marjorie Ste. Marie: First cousin to Judy (their mothers were sisters), she came to live with Judy and Judy's family when she was orphaned after her mother's death from pneumonia.

Clifford A. Taylor: Judy's husband

Cynthia (Cyndy) Taylor: Eldest daughter of Cliff and Judy

Julie Welburn: Middle daughter of Cliff and Judy

Miriam Taylor: Youngest daughter of Cliff and Judy

Glenna Taylor: Glenna was secretary at Trinity United Church and managed the volunteers' work in the office as the church grew and needed more help. Judy was one of those volunteers.

George Tsallas, BScPhm: A personal friend of our family, he was the pharmacist at TGH who became very involved in Judy's TPN solutions and became an integral part of Jeejeebhoy's team. His PhD paper provided me with much background knowledge.

Prof. Erik Vinnars, MD, PhD: Associate professor at St. Erik Hospital in Stockholm, he asked Judy to visit a female patient of his while she was visiting Sweden. (He is now deceased.)

Fern Waterman, MSc, MD: I spoke to Dr. Waterman, a psychiatrist, about the kinds of issues that come up when people cannot eat or have health crises.

Dorothy Webber: Her husband, Russell, did carpentry work on the Taylors' cottage to winterize it while Cliff was in the city. Dorothy belonged to the same UCW (United Church Women) group as Judy.

Prof. Arvid Wretlind, MD: The author of the foreword to this book, Prof. Wretlind was born on January 28, 1919, and he became a doctor of medicine in 1949 at the Karolinska Institute. He has published more than 275 papers relating to intravenous nutrition. In 1943, he developed a safe amino-acid preparation for intravenous infusion. From 1954 on, he worked on solving problems of intravenous fat emulsion, and he showed that a fat emulsion containing soybean oil, instead of cottonseed oil, was safe. He received the Swedish Royal Order Polar Star in 1962; the Swedish Royal Vasa Order in 1970; the Great Annual Gold Medal from the Royal Academy Engineering Sciences in Stockholm in 1979; Scientiae doctoris, Rutgers University, New Brunswick, NJ in 1980; and the Bristol-Myers Nutrition Award in 1985. (He is now deceased.)

John Wright, MD: Dr. Wright was junior resident in medicine from 1969 to 1970 and became involved in Judy's care during his senior residency from April to June 1971 (as a rule, new residents start on July 1).

Don Young: An American, he was Howard's second patient on TPN at the Albany Medical Center. He called Jeejeebhoy, who suggested he come up to

TGH so that he could meet with Jeejeebhoy and with others on TPN. He did so about three weeks after he was discharged. Don also spoke to Judy and met with her. Until the Oley Foundation Conference, he didn't see her again, but they spoke often on the phone.

W. John Zohrab, MB, BS: A resident in gastroenterology, he was working directly under Jeejeebhoy when Judy first arrived at TGH. He was a big part of her care.

Glossary

ACU	Acute Care Unit
Alimentation	Early form of total parenteral nutrition (TPN)
Amino acid	A basic constituent of protein. Some the body can synthesize; others known as essential amino acids, come only from food.
Ampicillin	An antibiotic
Anastomosis	A surgical connection between two normally separate parts
Appendicitis	Inflammation of the appendix, a small vestigial part attached to the cecum
Arteriovenous	Pertains to both an artery and a vein
Bronchoscopy	A method of examining the bronchi in the lungs, using a bronchoscope
Cecum	The first part of the large intestine or colon
Cellulitis	Inflammation of the soft or connective tissue due to infection
Central venous catheter	A catheter or plastic or silicone tubing with a small circumference that is placed in one of the large veins in the upper part of the body
Cephalic vein	A large vein in the upper arm
Cephosporin	An antibiotic
Cortisone	The synthetic form of the hormone that the adrenal cortex, part of the adrenal gland, secretes; there are two adrenal glands, and they sit near the kidneys

CPR	Cardiopulmonary resuscitation, a method used to revive a person from a cardiac or respiratory arrest
Cytokines	A group of proteins or peptides used by cells to talk to one another; many types of cells release cytokines, and cytokines are particularly important in the way the immune system responds to threats
Demerol®	See morphine
Detergicide™	A disinfectant, also used as an antiseptic back when Judy started using it
Dilaudid®	See morphine
Duodenum	The first part of the small intestine into which the stomach empties
Duodenal loop	The loop created when the surgeons cut out all of Judy's bowels; only a small stump of her duodenum was left, which they formed into a loop and closed off
ECG	Electrocardiogram, a tracing of the heart's rhythms
Edematous	Pertaining to edema, which is swelling of the tissues due to abnormally large quantities of fluid in the spaces between cells
Electrolytes	Elements, such as sodium, potassium, and chlorine, that maintain electrical and osmotic equilibrium, including fluid balance and electrical conduction in nerves and muscles
Emboli	Clots that have migrated to an organ
Endocrinologist	A specialist of the endocrine system, which is concerned with hormones
Excoriated	Loss of skin; an example is seen following non-stop scratching but is not the only cause
Fat emulsion	A solution that contains fat in small enough globules so as to appear homogeneous

Fistula	An abnormal passage between two organs or between an organ and the surface of the body
Fistulae	The plural form of fistula
Garamycin®	An antibiotic
Gastrostomy tube or G-tube	A tube that goes from the stomach through the abdominal wall to the outside; used to feed into the stomach or drain the stomach
Gastroenterologist or GI	A specialist of the digestive system
Gentamycin	An antibiotic
GP	General practitioner, the family doctor or family physician
Glucose	A simple sugar the body uses for energy
Graves' Disease	A disorder of the thyroid, marked by an increased secretion of the thyroid hormone, which results in an increased metabolic rate
Heparin	A drug that thins the blood
Hepatic artery	The artery that supplies blood to the liver
Hickman line	A central intravenous catheter (called "line") inserted through the chest wall into one of the major veins in the chest; central lines are larger than the peripheral IV lines inserted into the arms, hands, or feet
HPEN and HPENners	Home parenteral and enteral nutrition (HPENners are people who use these alternative methods of feeding. Parenteral refers to the method in which a catheter is permanently placed into a major vein in the chest, through which nutritional fluids are infused every night. Enteral refers to the method in which a person receives through a tube placed in the stomach or intestine a pre-digested liquid, instead of consuming food.)
Hydrocephalus	Dilatation of the cerebral ventricles, usually caused by obstruction of the flow of cerebrospinal fluid

Hygroscopic	The ready absorption and retention of moisture
Hyperalimentation	The first incarnation of TPN (total parenteral nutrition)
Hyperkinetic bone turnover	This is faster-than-normal absorption and rebuilding of the bones
Hypertension	High blood pressure
Hyperthyroidism	See Graves' Disease above
Hypotension	Low blood pressure
Ileum	The lower part of the small intestine extending from the jejunum to the cecum
Interstitial	In the spaces between tissues (An IV needle that goes interstitial is one that has come out of the blood vessel and is lodged in the surrounding tissue.)
Intralipid®	A fat emulsion developed in Sweden by Prof. Arvid Wretlind using soybean oil as the source of fat
Ischemic	Pertains to an insufficiency of blood flow
L-thyroxin	A synthetic form of thyroxine, a hormone secreted by the thyroid
Laparotomy	A surgical procedure that allows access to the abdominal cavity
Linoleic acid	An omega-6 fatty acid, a polyunsaturated fat that is an essential fatty acid, meaning it's only available from dietary sources because the body cannot synthesize it
Lifeliner	A person who lives on TPN
Mesenteric vein	This vein takes blood away from the intestines (the superior mesenteric from the small intestine, the inferior from the colon)
Methacholine	A drug that stimulates the parasympathetic nervous system

Morphine	A narcotic which is used to reduce the perception of pain but has other action similar to the effect of opium
MSOF	Multisystem organ failure; an infection, the catalyst of MSOF, is usually killed by doctors, but starts a process that back in 1991 killed the victim 80 percent of the time
Myelin sheath	Covers the long part of the neuron and acts as an electrical insulator; it enhances the conductivity of the cell and is made up mostly of fats
Necrosis	Tissue or cell death
Nephrology	Study of the kidneys
Neurology	Study of the nervous system, including the brain
NG tube	Nasogastric tube (It is inserted through the nose and threaded down the esophagus into the stomach.)
Omentum	A curtain of fat that sits under the stomach
Omeprazole (Losec®)	A drug used to treat gastrointestinal illnesses such as peptic ulcer disease
Osmotic pressure	The force that moves salts and water between salt solutions of differing concentrations in contact with each other so as to equilibrate the concentrations difference between two; water moves from the area of lesser salt concentration to one of greater
Osteoid seam	Area of uncalcified bone
Osteomalacia	A softening of the bones, usually from a deficiency of vitamin D and calcium
Ovarian cyst	A cyst, or closed sac filled with liquid, in the ovary
Parathyroid hormone	Hormone produced by the parathyroid gland, which is situated beside the thyroid gland and is involved in the metabolism of calcium and phosphorus

Penrose drain	Named after Charles Bingham Penrose, a Philadelphia gynecologist who lived from 1862 to 1925; it drains pus and infected material out of the body
Peripheral neuropathy	Functional disturbances in the peripheral nerves, those nerves that branch out from the central nervous system and end in the skin layer
Peptide	Comprises two or more amino acids and forms the constituent parts of proteins
Pericholangitis	Inflammation of the tissues that surround the bile duct
Peritoneum	The membrane that lines the inside of the abdomen and covers all the viscera inside
Peritonitis	Inflammation of the peritoneum
Pleura	The membrane that lines the inside of the chest and covers the lungs
Protein hydrolysate	A mixture of amino acids, which are derived by chemically or enzymatically heating a protein
Pseudo-obstruction	A condition that simulates physical obstruction of the intestine
Pulmonary	Having to do with the lungs
Pulmonary emboli	Clots in the lungs
Pulmonary vascular congestion	Congestion of the blood vessels in the lungs
Pylorospasm	A spasm of the part of the stomach through which digested food empties into the duodenum, the first section of the small intestine
Respirologist	A specialist who deals with the respiratory or breathing system
RNA	Registered nursing assistant
RN	Registered nurse

Sepsis	A generalized infection (The bacterial toxins in a septic person secrete cytokines, which dilate the blood vessels, change the permeability of the capillaries' walls so that they leak, and cause widespread damage to the major organs. If sepsis isn't brought under control, it can lead to multisystem organ failure, MSOF.)
Septicemia	Bacteria proliferating in the bloodstream
Silastic®	Trademarked term for polymeric silicone substances that are like rubber and are biologically inert
Shunt	An artificial structure that connects two blood vessels
Soluzyme	A vitamin solution used in TPN
Splenic artery	The artery that supplies blood to the spleen
Subclavian vein	The large vein that is situated under the clavicle and drains blood from the arm to the heart
Tachycardia	High heart rate or racing of the heart
Talwin®	A narcotic
TGH	Toronto General Hospital
Thrombosis	Formation of a clot in a blood vessel
Thiouracyl tablets	A drug that blocks the synthesis of thyroid hormones
Thyroxine	A drug that mimics the hormone secreted by the thyroid gland, which is involved in regulating the metabolic rate
Tobramycin	An antibiotic
Torsion	A twist that results in blood supply being cut off
TPN	Total parenteral nutrition, a technology that allows a person to live entirely without eating by supplying all needed nutrients in liquid form through a central catheter permanently placed in a large vein in the neck or chest.
Ulnar vein	A vein that drains blood from the side of the forearm opposite to that of the thumb

Ultrasound, Abdominal Refers to taking "sound pictures" of all of the organs in the abdomen, or the area below the ribs (Using sound waves bouncing off of tissue, an ultrasound operator can take pictures of the internal organs.)

Xanthelasma A yellow plaque or spots on the eyelid

Bibliography

This is a list of the English-language journal articles, newspaper articles, and books that I read as background research plus a few more that you may find interesting.

Scribner, B., J. Cole, T. Christopher, J. Vizzo, R. Atkins, and C. Blagg. 1970. Long-term total parenteral nutrition. The concept of an artificial gut. *JAMA* 212:457–463.

Tsallas, G., and D. Baun. 1972. Home care total parenteral alimentation. *Am J Hosp Pharm* 29:840–846.

Zohrab, W. J., J. McHattie, and K. Jeejeebhoy. 1973. Total parenteral alimentation with lipid. *Gastroenterology* 64(4):583–592.

Jeejeebhoy, K., W. J. Zohrab, and B. Langer. 1973. Total parenteral nutrition at home for 23 months sans complications and with good rehab. *Gastroenterology* 65(5):811–820.

Langer, B., J. McHattie, W. J. Zohrab, and K. Jeejeebhoy. 1973. Prolonged survival after complete small bowel resection using intravenous alimentation at home. *J Surg Res* 15(3):226–233.

Jeejeebhoy, K. 1974. Long-term parenteral nutrition. *Gastroenterology* 67(1):196–197 (reply to letter).

Jeejeebhoy, K., G. H. Anderson, I. Sanderson, and M. Bryan. 1974. Total parenteral nutrition: nutrient needs and technical tips. *Modern Med Canada* 29: (part 1) September 832–841 and (part 2) October 944–947.

Jeejeebhoy, K., G. H. Anderson, F. Nakhooda, and G. Greenberg et al. 1976. Metabolic studies in total parenteral nutrition with lipid in man: comparison with glucose. *J Clin Invest* 57:125–136.

Jeejeebhoy, K., B. Langer, G. Tsallas, R. Chu, A. Kuksis, and G. H. Anderson. 1976. Total parenteral nutrition at home: studies in patients surviving 4 months to 5 years. *Gastroenterology* 71(6):943–953.

Jeejeebhoy, K. 1976. Total parenteral nutrition (TPN)—a review. *Ann R Coll Phys Surg Canada* 9:287–300.

Jeejeebhoy, K. 1976. Total parenteral nutrition (TPN) at home. *Can J Surg* 19:477–478 (editorial).

Jeejeebhoy, K., R. Chu, E. Marliss, G. Greenberg, and A. Bruce-Robertson. 1977. Chromium deficiency, glucose intolerance, and neuropathy reversed by chromium supplementation, in a patient receiving long-term total parenteral nutrition. *Am J Clin Nutr* 30(4):531–538.

MacRitchie, K. J. 1978. Life without eating or drinking. Total parenteral nutrition outside hospital. *Can Psychiatr Assoc J* 23:373–379.

Wolman, S., G. H. Anderson, E. Marliss, and K. Jeejeebhoy. 1979. Zinc in total parenteral nutrition: requirements and metabolic effects. *Gastroenterology* 76(3):458–467.

Jeejeebhoy, K. 1979. Is more better? Is weight water? The significance of weight gain during parenteral nutrition with amino acids and dextrose. *Gastroenterology* 77(4):799–800 (editorial).

Jeejeebhoy, K., and B. Langer. 1980. Home parenteral nutrition. *Can Med Assoc J* 122:143–144.

Shike, M., J. Harrison, W. Sturtridge, C. Tam, P. Bobechko, G. Jones, T. Murray, and K. Jeejeebhoy. 1980. Metabolic bone disease in patients receiving long-term total parenteral nutrition. *Ann Int Med* 92(3):343–350.

Izsak, E., M. Shike, M. Roulet, and K. Jeejeebhoy. 1980. Pancreatitis in association with hypercalcemia in patients receiving total parenteral nutrition. *Gastroenterology* 79(3):555–558.

Glynn, M., B. Langer, and K. Jeejeebhoy. 1980. Therapy for thrombotic occlusion of long-term intravenous alimentation catheters. *JPEN* 4(4):387–390.

Mernagh, J., K. McNeill, J. Harrison, and K. Jeejeebhoy. 1981. Effect of total parenteral nutrition in the restitution of body nitrogen, potassium and weight. *Nutr Res* 1(2):149–157.

Shike, M., W. Sturtridge, C. Tam, J. Harrison, G. Jones, T. Murray, H. Husdan, J. Whitwell, D. Wilson, and K. Jeejeebhoy. 1981. A possible role of vitamin D in the genesis of parenteral-nutrition-induced metabolic bone disease. *Ann Int Med* 95(5):560–568.

Greig P., J. Baker, and K. Jeejeebhoy. 1982. Metabolic effects of total parenteral nutrition. *Ann Rev Nutr* 2:179–199.

Jeejeebhoy, K. ed. with the assistance of A. Bruce-Robertson. *Total Parenteral Nutrition in the Hospital and at Home.* Boca Raton: CRC Press, Inc. 1983.

Shike, M., and K. Jeejeebhoy. 1983. Copper nutriture in total parenteral nutrition. *Clin Nutr* 2(3):5–7.

Jeejeebhoy, K., and M. Shike. 1983. Aluminum and metabolic bone disease. *Ann Int Med* 99(5):733–734 (letters and corrections).

Jeejeebhoy, K. 1984. Zinc and chromium in parenteral nutrition. *Bull NY Acad Med* 60(2):118–124.

McGee, C., M. Mascarenhas, M. Ostro, G. Tsallas, and K. Jeejeebhoy. 1985. Selenium and vitamin E stability in parenteral solutions. *JPEN* 9(5):568–570.

Jeejeebhoy, K. 1986. Trace element requirements during TPN. *Nutritional Support Services* 6(5):16–17.

Detsky, A., J. McLaughlin, H. Abrams, K. L'Abbe, J. Whitwell, C. Bombardier, and K. Jeejeebhoy. 1986. Quality of life of patients on long-term total parenteral nutrition at home. *J Gen Int Med* 1:26–33.

Jeejeebhoy, K. 1987. Parenteral nutrition. *Curr Opin Gastroenterology* 3(2):313–320.

Jeejeebhoy, K. 1988. Parenteral nutrition. *Curr Opin Gastroenterology* 4:306–314.

Lemoyne, M., A. Van Gossum, R. Kurian, and K. Jeejeebhoy. 1988. Plasma vitamin E and selenium and breath pentane in home parenteral nutrition patients. *Am J Clin Nutr* 48:1310–1315.

Wakefield, A., Z. Cohen, M. Craig, P. Connolley, K. Jeejeebhoy, R. Silverman, and G. Levy. 1989. Thrombogenicity of total parenteral nutrition solutions: I. Effect on induction of monocyte/macrophage procoagulant activity. *Gastroenterology* 97(5):1210–1219.

Wakefield, A., Z. Cohen, A. Rosenthal, M. Craig, K. Jeejeebhoy, A. Gotlieb, and G. Levy. 1989. Thrombogenicity of total parenteral nutrition solutions: II. Effect on induction of endothelial cell procoagulant activity. *Gastroenterology* 97(5):1220–1228.

Jeejeebhoy, K. 1990. Does twice a week lipid infusion prevent essential fatty acid (EFA) deficiency during total parenteral nutrition (TPN)? *Nutrition* 6(2):193 (editorial).

Abstracts and Theses

Zohrab, W., B. Langer, and K. Jeejeebhoy. 1972. Total parenteral alimentation at home. In: Abstracts of short communications published by the Ninth International Congress of Nutrition, Mexico City, Mexico, p. 19.

Patel, D., G. H. Anderson, and K. Jeejeebhoy. 1972. Comparative evaluation of the sources of nitrogen for parenteral alimentation using nitrogen balance and blood aminogram. In: Abstracts of short communications published by the Ninth International Congress of Nutrition, Mexico City, Mexico, p. 79.

Tsallas, G. 1972. An analysis of the hyperalimentation programme at Toronto General Hospital for the period March 1971–March 1972. Toronto: [s.n.]. Submitted in partial fulfillment of the requirements for the Hospital Pharmacy Residency Certificate.

Jeejeebhoy, K., and B. Langer. 1973. A home care programme for total parenteral nutrition(TPN). *Gastroenterology* 64(4):750.

McDonald, A. T. J., M. J. Phillips, and K. Jeejeebhoy. 1973. Reversal of fatty liver by Intralipid in patients on total parenteral alimentation. *Gastroenterology* 64(4–6):885.

Jeejeebhoy, K., R. Chu, E. Marliss, G. Greenberg, and A. Bruce-Robertson. 1975. Chromium deficiency, diabetes and neuropathy, reversed by chromium infusion in a patient on total parenteral nutrition (TPN) for 3–1/2 years. *Clin Res* 23(5):636A.

Jeejeebhoy, K., B. Langer, G. Greenberg, K. Ng, and P. Little. 1976. Total parenteral nutrition: a five-year survival at home. *Ann R Coll Phys Surg Can* 9(1):38 (Abstr #80).

Jones, G., B. Byrnes, and K. Jeejeebhoy. 1979. Contribution of skin vitamin D3 synthesis in patients receiving total parenteral nutrition. Presented in program of fourth workshop on Vitamin D, February, in Berlin, West Germany.

Shike, M., W. Sturtridge, J. Harrison, C. Tam, and K. Jeejeebhoy. 1979. Bone disease in patients receiving long-term parenteral nutrition (TPN). *Am J Clin Nutr* 32(6):20 (Abstr #16).

Shike, M., R. Kurian, M. Roulet, S. Stewart, J. Whitwell, and K. Jeejeebhoy. 1980. Copper (Cu) requirements in total parenteral nutrition (TPN). *Gastroenterology* 78(5):1259.

Shike, M., W. Sturtridge, J. Harrison, C. Tam, G. Jones, J. Whitwell, T. Murray, D. Wilson, and K. Jeejeebhoy. 1980. The role of vitamin D in the etiology of metabolic bone disease in patients receiving long-term parenteral nutrition. *JPEN* 4(6):585 (Abstr #18).

McNeill, K. G., J. Harrison, J. Mernagh, S. Stewart, and K. Jeejeebhoy. 1980. Changes in body protein, body potassium and lean body mass during total parenteral nutrition (TPN). *JPEN* 4(6):588 (Abstr #32).

Greig, P., S. Stewart, S. Wolman, Z. Cohen, B. Langer, and K. Jeejeebhoy. 1986. Fifteen years of adult home parenteral nutrition. *Clin Invest Med* 9(3):(Suppl)A53 (Abstr #R-325).

Close, M., and K. Jeejeebhoy. 1986. Personal control and life satisfaction among home total parenteral (HPN) patients. *Clin Nutr* 5(Special Suppl Sept):113 (Abstr #P33).

Newspaper and Magazine Articles

Hollobon, Joan. 1972. Woman cooks for her family, but she's fed through 'lifeline.' *The Globe and Mail*, April 20. (I got a copy of this article from Judy's files, and the person who clipped it out for her wrote "your [sic] famous!" in black with a big arrow pointing to the article.)

Trent, Bill. 1974. A Life Without Food. *Weekend Magazine*, June 22.

Hollobon, Joan. 1976. Chromium in diet may play role in diabetes, scientist says. *The Globe and Mail*, January 22.

Hynes, Mary. 1982. Patients can't eat, but live. *The Globe and Mail*, June 4.

Howell, Peter. 1988. Judy lives 18 foodless years—grateful for every second. *Toronto Star*, December 21.

Jimison, Susan. 1989. Woman hasn't eaten a bite in 19 years! *Weekly World News*, February 7.

Paterson, Gladys. 1989. Toronto patient "Judy" a true survivor. *Seniors Today*, May 10.

978-0-595-44544-8
0-595-44544-6

Printed in the United States
95218LV00004B/1-159/A